SHIFTING GEARS

A Journey of Reinvention

MARI PINTKOWSKI

iUniverse, Inc.
Bloomington

Shifting Gears
A Journey of Reinvention

iUniverse books may be ordered through booksellers or by contacting:

iUniverse
1663 Liberty Drive
Bloomington, IN 47403
www.iuniverse.com
1-800-Authors (1-800-288-4677)

ISBN: 978-1-4620-1735-5 (sc)
ISBN: 978-1-4620-1740-9 (dj)
ISBN: 978-1-4620-1739-3 (ebook)

Printed in the United States of America

iUniverse rev. date: 05/23/2011

For Lou, together we're better

Special thanks to my editor and mentor, Murray Laurie
And to Bertha Campbell and Trudy Johnson for their guidance

TABLE OF CONTENTS

"The magic of stories is often an important road for traveling through reality and imagination, for encountering culture and life, for knowing and interpreting the world around us."

"The Circle of Words,"
Reggio Emilia Early Childhood Centers
2008

INTRODUCTION

They say love makes you do crazy things and writing your love story is an example. In order to do this you must first dig deep into your soul and find out just who you are before you can truly understand another.

Shifting Gears: A Journey of Reinvention is a story of two people with separate voices who merge together in mid-life, then take a short pause along the road, and when the time is right, they make a conscious choice to build a life together.

The tenses I use to tell our story shift between the present and past for emphasis.

The journey begins in present tense in the B & B my husband and I have built near Tulum, Mexico. We start to reflect on the passage of turning sixty; how we have reinvented our life and where we will get the inspiration for the next sixty years.

Pedaling Toward Sixty
Time to Pack for the Pacific Northwest

Stories are the magic element I use to build an image of my Polish-American husband, from his childhood to his formative years as a ski bum in the classy towns of Vail and Aspen in the 1970s, 80s and 90s before settling in as my partner in the mid-90s in Vail and finally in our *casa* in Mexico. Thirty-five photos help bring the stories to life.

During the gap in our relationship in 1995, Lou embarks on a journey of a lifetime; a solo, two-and-half month bicycle trip from Steamboat Springs, Colorado, north to the National Parks of the west, across the Cascade mountains to the Pacific Northwest, and down the Pacific coast where his bike journey ends in Palm Springs, California, before returning to my daughter and me in Colorado. His humorous voice is loud and clear as he pedals along pulling out stories from the past to introduce people and places he visits on his tour.

The Launch: Back on the Road
Adventures in Big Sky Country
Heading for the Far North
Kalispell, Whitefish and Places Beyond
Riding the Rails to the Pacific Ocean
In the Saddle Again
Island Fever
Wheeling through Northwest Canada
Back in the USA
Riding to the Rainforest
California, Here I Come

Perched on the seat of his bicycle, he has unlimited time to reflect and put the pieces of his life together and begin to dream about the future.

Meeting the Past, Facing the Future
Recovering and Reuniting
Staying on Course

My voice returns as I narrate how our life together has shifted over the years.

Seven Years Later: The Wedding
The Third Thing
South of the Border

When we embark on the return trip to the Pacific Northwest to retrace Lou's footsteps from his bike journey thirteen years before, Lou is no longer on a solo journey and I have become the storyteller seeing the Northwest with new eyes.

Traveling in Tandem
North to the Border

Pacific Northwest

The biographical story ends with me reflecting on how my Polish American, jack-of all-trades husband has changed since his youth and the solo bike journey he made once-upon-a-time.

Following the Mariposa Trail

Lou has included the details of his bike adventure in the *Appendix: Lou Reflects*

PEDDALING TOWARD SIXTY

one

My Polish-American, jack-of-all-trades husband and I are turning sixty this year. The upcoming passage has led to much discussion and reflection of what we want to accomplish in our lives and just how our past has influenced our thinking.

One steamy night under a whirling fan in our *casa* in Mexico, we begin to talk about the path we have chosen that led us to a foreign country, many miles from friends and family, simply allowing the elusive butterfly to guide us as we traveled south from Vail, Colorado, to Tulum three years ago. I smile slightly as I begin to speak to Lou, "Where are you going to get the inspiration for the next sixty years of your life?"

He disappears upstairs and comes back carrying a large, white plastic box. I recognize it as one of Lou's treasured possessions that has survived the many moves he has made in his adult life. He lovingly sets the box on the table and taps the top with his knuckles. He slowly opens the lid and whispers, "I have opened this box on occasion in the past when I needed inspiration, confidence, optimism and joy."

"Sounds like this is a good time to revisit what's inside, Lou."

I sit uncharacteristically still as he speaks with the air of a storyteller.

"The pictures and news clippings from my youth bring back memories that awaken the stories in my mind," Lou says solemnly.

As he hands me the first picture, his description begins to transcend the barriers of time and space and makes me feel like I am with him as

1

he is running down Vail Mountain. His lean five-foot-eight frame had a bronze glow, hinting that being outdoors was more than an occasional happening. He leans over and explains, "What's not in the picture is that I am betting my ski-buddies that I can run down Vail Mountain from Mid-Vail and beat the gondola to the bottom."

"Lou, you said you were betting against your buddies. Tell me more."

"What else did one do in the summer in the small ski town of Vail in 1967 except sit on the Red Lion deck sucking down a few beers while watching the gondola go up and down? One of our favorite topics in the winter at *après ski* was how many runs you made from the top of the mountain to the bottom that day. This made me remember how my thighs burned non-stop down Riva Ridge and how good it felt to push myself to be the first to arrive at the lift."

"Sounds like a bit of boasting, or beer talk to me."

"Maybe, but we all knew that the only thing that limited the number of runs we could make in a day was the speed of the lifts. That's when I got the stupid idea that I could run faster than that silver bubble that traveled up and down the mountain on its cable. Of course, now we had to find out. We were all in a state of anticipation when we boarded the next gondola car to Mid-Vail."

"The intense expression on your face in the photo tells me this was more than fun and games for you. What's the rest of the story? I want to know more."

Lou explains that in his youth, he had an obsession for challenging his strengths against himself and others. "More often than not, I didn't think about the physical damage that I could, and often did endure during these challenges. On that particular day, we rode the gondola up to Mid-Vail, and after placing our bets, I headed down the mountain at a pace I thought I could maintain while keeping an eye on the gondola car that my friends were riding in. I was trying my best to keep up. It did not take long to realize there was no way I could beat the gondola unless there was one of the all-too-common power outages. No such luck! Do you think that I gave up and took the catwalk around the grueling *Pepi's Face* which later became the finish line of many international ski events? No, instead I went straight down the mountain to the base where I knew my *amigos* would be watching from the Red Lion deck.

When I got down the mountain, all I could think of were my screaming knees and burning thighs that kept me limping for days."

"I bet everyone still cheered you on and toasted with a cold beer in hand even though you failed at the attempt. Lou I can't help but ask, was this about them or you?"

"I would have to say a little of both, but I think it was more about the feeling of satisfaction I got from pushing myself to the limit than pleasing the crowd."

I set the picture down on the table, and wonder what I would have done. In minutes Lou hands me another photo. This one is smaller with scalloped edges and is almost a sepia color. I have to adjust the light to see that it is Lou as a young boy proudly standing in front of his family's brick-front house on Packard Street in what is now a suburb of Detroit, Michigan. His hand rests proudly on a Schwinn Hornet bicycle. "That's a beauty, Lou. It is bigger than you are. Did you get it for your birthday or something?"

"It was a hand-me-down from my brother, and my sister before him. I wasn't proud! I was elated to finally have wheels. This gave me the opportunity to reach beyond my immediate neighborhood and finally be able to explore the boondocks like my older siblings. I will never forget the exhilarating feeling I had on my first ride as I took off from my house and eventually bumped down a dirt road all by myself. In fact, Moe, the bike gave me the opportunity to earn money with my paper route."

I think back to my youth and respond, "I remember when my brother had a paper route. It was a lot of responsibility, but I don't recall that it was much of an adventure."

Lou sits down and a very serious look crosses his face. "I had the best corner in my neighborhood for the Sunday papers and I even took on a helper and had him delivering the papers on my regular two routes. I know this sounds crazy for a twelve year old, but I would get up at 4 a.m. on Sundays and go to the coffee shop across the street from my corner and order toast and coffee while I waited for the bundles of the Sunday edition of the Detroit Free Press and The Detroit News to be dropped off."

"Are you serious? I am surprised your family let you do this and miss the ritual of attending Mass together."

"I guess it was because I was earning money that my dad gave me permission to skip church. In fact, I remember how my family would drive by my corner at 10 a.m. after Mass and honk the horn."

"Perhaps your Dad knew this was something you felt strongly about and he wanted to support you as a parent. I try to do this with my daughter Ailish when I can."

"I was never satisfied with the norm. I had to push myself to do more. I guess I was always trying to prove my worth to my parents, my older siblings and their friends because I was younger and smaller. I was the kid who always got picked last to play ball and got sent out to cover right field."

"I think as an adult you often challenge yourself as well."

"I am trying to be more tranquil these days and not let my ego control my actions. However, I often took the opposite approach in the many business ventures I engaged in and, as you know, it was not always successful; but that is a story for another night."

"Lou, did you bike in the early days when you lived in Vail?"

"Sure, but I didn't have a good bike until I moved to Aspen several years later. In the early 1970s, the Celestial Seasonings Amateur-Pro Race was scheduled to take place in Vail, and the town race committee wanted to get the locals involved in the events so they set up preliminary races to test the course."

"I remember those races when I arrived in Vail in the summer of 1975. My first husband, Dan, and I had recently settled in Vail and were not part of the local scene yet, so we joined the many spectators cheering the racers on as they cycled through the tight curves on Mill Creek Circle. I always wanted to have one of the classic T-shirts the racers wore. Any chance there is one in that white box of yours?" He didn't even have a photo or newspaper clipping of the sporting event, but his description of that day was told in the kind of detail that could have come out of the *Vail Trail* newspaper.

"I could not afford a good bike and would not attempt the event with any of the beat-up bikes my friends owned, so I did the next best thing. I knew a retired pro-bike racer, Caesar Moretti, who owned a ski shop in the village where he built, sold and rented bicycles in the summer. I approached him with the challenge to train me for the preliminaries using one of his professional road bikes."

"Tell me more about this bike racer, and if you had any luck getting a bike to use in the race."

"I recall that Caesar was a tall, thin man in his forties with a chiseled face who hailed from Italy. As I said before, there wasn't a lot, even for a shop owner, to do in the summer in Vail. He thought this was a fine idea, and he thought the word of mouth advertising that was the norm in those days might place the name of his shop in the public eye."

Lou goes on to explain how he and Caesar worked together for a few weeks. I drift off a bit and am imagining Lou in a Celestial Seasonings jersey with the logo of Caesar's bike shop silk screened on the back as he approaches the start of the ten-lap race with pride and a bit of cockiness. Lou sets me straight that there were no jerseys, not even T-shirts, which he could remember for this test run for the racecourse.

Lou had a lot of respect for Caesar and his past history as a bike racer, but Lou's ego got the best of him. Instead of following the instructions of his coach to hold back at the start, Lou took the lead and tried his best to remain there. Lou's competitive drive would not let him be anywhere but in the front of the pack from the get-go. He was in the lead until the last two laps when his energy was totally depleted and the other racers began to sprint and overtook my Polish-American athlete.

"Wow! I see what your coach meant by not taking the lead at the start of the race. Did you ever compete in the Celestial Seasonings races in Vail the following years? "

"Hell no, Moe, I was not that strong of a racer or climber to be competing against the world's best. I kept my eyes on much weaker targets."

He handed me a photo and said, "Take a look at this one of me and the bike I had built by one of the shops in the village the year I moved to Aspen. I actually paid $1,000 for it, which was quite a hefty price to pay for a recreational bicycle in the early 70s."

"Lou, what was so special about this bluish-purple bicycle that it cost $1,000?"

"The bike was a beauty. It was a Gueciotti made in Italy and was one of the lightest- weight frames you could purchase at that time. I had learned from Caesar about the importance of having a bicycle that was specifically geared to your skills and needs. I let the shop that was building the bike for me know that I would be using it primarily to ride up and down mountain passes and that I was not that strong a climber. There was no such thing on the market as a mountain bike in those days, so my riding took place on the winding roads leading in and out of Aspen."

"Did your interest in bike racing escalate or did you have other plans for that gorgeous piece of equipment?"

"At first the bike was used totally for relaxation and entertainment. Even when my life was centered on partying until the wee hours, I always had the motivation to get up on many a crisp Colorado morning and take off on my bike for a ride out to Maroon Bells, or Independence Pass. The breathtaking scenery of tall snow-covered mountain peaks, pencil-thin aspen trees with leaves quivering in the wind and a palate of color from the wildflowers that bloom during the short summer season still stay in my memory. Riding the back roads to places you go to *be*, rather than to *be seen,* was what was rejuvenating to me in those days.

Remember that enduring-sameness that was the norm in ski towns in the summer of the '70s? We had to create our own entertainment because there was no signal for television or radio in those days in the high country and only a weekly newspaper to connect us with the outside world."

"Do I hear a hint of longing in your voice, Lou?"

"To tell you the truth, Moe, that is the thing I miss the most about living in Mexico; riding my bike on roads that twist and turn with a photo-op around every corner."

Lou rummages through the box for awhile, stopping to glance at the photos and newspaper clippings until he finds what he is looking for. His eyes are animated as he glances at the photo. I get the feeling there is going to be a great story to go with this one. "Moe, you're going to love this."

He passes the photo tenderly over to me and I exclaim, "For heaven's sake, why are you carrying your bicycle on your back?"

"It all started at the end of a long day at the Aspen Mine Company where I worked as general manager of the restaurant. One of the young, boastful waiters did not believe that I, an older gentleman of thirty, could keep up with the younger crowd on a bike ride. We continued to one-up each other as we told stories of our conquests on the mountain roads surrounding Aspen. We eventually made a $1,000 wager to race on our bikes to the top of Maroon Bells campground from Aspen and back again. We also included a no-show agreement of $250, if either of us decided to withdraw from the race."

"Lou, I recall that Maroon Bells was quite a distance from the town of Aspen."

"Well, it was only twelve miles from town and, although uphill all the way; it was a pretty easy twenty-four-mile road ride."

"Funny that you should mention Maroon Bells, I actually have a photo of myself from a 1970 road trip with my girl friends taken in front of that very lake with the two, towering peaks reflected in the glassy surface of the water."

"I'd love to see that one," Lou says with a smile. "I am not surprised. I have heard that the Maroon Bells, in the White River National Forest, is the most photographed peak in all of North America."

"That's interesting. What else do you know about those two peaks in the Elk Mountains?"

"Well they are both over 14,000 feet high, and are composed of sedimentary mudstone which has a tendency to flake and slide off the side of the mountain. When I was living in Aspen, several climbers died in a climbing accident on the mountain so it was nicknamed, "The Deadly Bells." That's enough geology for today Moe; now back to the story.'

"As I mentioned before, it was only twenty-four miles. I knew I needed an edge, something that could separate the men from the boys, so I proposed that once we reach Maroon Bells, we then run down carrying our bikes. Bob, being younger, felt he could outride and outrun his boss, so the bet was on."

"The race was set for a Monday. On the previous Friday I decided to do a pretest on my own. The photo was actually taken by Janet, one of my good friends who had come along that afternoon for moral support."

"Is that the same Janet we spent a few holidays with in our early dating days?"

"Yes, she and I go way back."

We both glance at the photo, and Lou continues. "As you can see, it was not one of those cobalt-blue Colorado days; instead the clouds cast long shadows on the cliffs above me. I did make it to the bottom and learned that I needed to make a few adjustments in the backpack-style harness I had fashioned to carry the bike. I added some padding to the crossbar and devised a new way to carry the bike on my shoulder by bracing it against my neck. I know it sounds a little crazy, but it actually worked and I made it to the bottom where Janet was waiting with her camera to snap a photo. The day of the race arrived and Bob showed up at the starting point without his bike and handed me $250 to forfeit the race. He had heard about my trial run and decided I was no match for him."

I sit for a few minutes with the photo in my hand. Lou, sitting across from me with laughter rising hysterically in his throat, lets me know that the funniest part was the comments the hikers he passed along the way made as he came running down the mountain road carrying his bicycle on the day of the training run.

The invitation to match skills and strength made at a bar late one night sounded like one of those events that we look forward to with great anticipation and then the event itself turns out to be different from what we expect, so much so that it becomes a new experience all together. There is nothing in Lou's joyful, intrepid stories that is remotely similar to anything that happened to me during my youth or, in fact to anyone else I had met thus far in my life. I had always known that my Polish-American husband was one-of-a-kind.

He starts to close the white box when I stop him; "Lou that was a great story. I cannot believe that you do not have more to tell."

"Moe, there are enough stories in this box to write a book about. I continued to create or get myself involved in competitive situations that included one event or another for quite a few years, but that's enough tales for tonight."

I beg him to tell me just one more as I sip the last of my wine beneath the slow-turning fan that moves the humid air above our heads. He pulls out a newspaper clipping and stares at me with renewed vigor. "I have to say that I saved the best story for last! It was during the mid-seventies that the camaraderie among Fred Angelo, Ron Riley and myself was at high pitch. One-upmanship was the game we played when it came to wine, women and sport."

"I think I remember at least one of these guys. Can you describe them for me?"

"Fred was one of those great people you sometimes get lucky to meet in your life. Sadly, he died a few years ago in Alaska. He stood about six foot tall and reflected the naturally good looks of his Italian ancestors. His dark, thick moustache was neatly clipped and he maintained a trim physique. He was part owner of the Gondola Ski Shop in Vail and another that was soon to open in Aspen. He was always married to one gorgeous woman or another. Fred had a fun-loving nature. He dazzled me with his gift as a master storyteller. I admired his ability to handle himself in any situation with anyone from the President of the United States, Gerald Ford, who frequented Vail at this time to the ski bums who hovered around Donovan's Copper Bar."

"Lou, I remember when he died, and do wish I had known the gentleman. He sounds like one of the many characters that Vail was known for in the 70s."

Lou continues, "Then there was Ron Riley. He was my boss as well as my *amigo*. He was the successful owner of a chain of restaurants and a real estate developer. Unlike Fred, Ron stood a bit closer to the ground with his five-foot-nine-inch stocky, muscular build. His face was round and a bit pudgy. He often sported a sly grin which drew the ski bunnies to his side. Ron always had a story to tell and an audience to cheer him on. Like Fred, he was comfortable with any kind of crowd."

"Stop, Lou! I know Ron pretty well. His little twins came to my school whenever they were in Vail. He and his family were living in Denver at the time. So knowing two out of three of the competitors is not bad. On with the story! "

"The plan began to take shape over dinner at one of Aspen's hip restaurants where we were inclined to run up quite a tab drinking expensive wine followed by Grand Marnier. The scenario that was beginning to spin out of control was centered on which of us was the best all-around jock. The seed was planted and we would soon find out!"

"Fred was the finesse man. Ron was versatile and talented in many areas. My strong card had always been endurance and persistence in solo sports."

"Over that bottle of Grand Marnier, we came up with the idea of staging a fifteen-event decathlon. The wager was set at $1,000 apiece; the winner would take all. This threesome found the prospect irresistible. Each of us chose five separate events and one alternate just in case we could not get the equipment or location worked out for one of them. You were responsible for providing the equipment and venue for your five events. When needed, there would be an official timekeeper or referee. We even wound up having John Atkinson following us around with his video camera taping many of the competitions."

"That is amazing Lou! Don't tell me you have the video tape in the white box?"

"No, Ron ended up with the video tape, but I have a photo showing me covered with dirt after the motocross race. I am saving it to show you after I finish the story."

"Before you go on, I have some questions? What were some of the events? Did they take place in Vail or Aspen? And just how long did the competition run?" I felt like I was a reporter for the *Vail Trail* newspaper.

"There was a putting contest, an archery shoot, a 10-mile bike race, a speed ice- skating event, a swimming meet, a rope climbing competition, barrel racing and the motocross race, to name a few. We went back and forth from Vail to Aspen over a six-week period in whichever place the event could best be organized. We even had a following. We used a point system: five points for the winner, three points for runner-up and one point for the loser of the match."

"That sounds like a clever idea," I said.

"Well, it worked great for this little sporting event. By the time we got to the final match, the motocross race, Fred had dropped out and became the timekeeper, and the competition was between Ron and me. I remember feeling a bit irritated because we had to run the motocross event three times because Fred kept claiming it was a tie. When the dust had settled the last time around, I was proclaimed the winner. The $3,000 pot was awarded to yours truly. Now you can see the photo, Moe."

"Frankly, I am surprised this competition never made it into the local newspaper.

But maybe some things are best kept away from public scrutiny."

Lou sits back with his arms loosely folded on his chest, shoulders pushed up in a peaceful shrug and his crossed ankles rest on the coffee table. There is a hammock-shaped smile partly hidden beneath his graying beard.

I am stunned as I linger over the photo of my young, intrepid hero. "That was amazing. You never gave up and, most of all you proved that you could succeed when the going got tough."

I stretch out on the couch and quietly say, "Lou, I notice that one thing these stories have in common with how you live your life today is that you always push yourself to go further than you think you can."

"That's right, Moe. I find that mentally and physically invigorating. I love the feeling of being really tired after stretching myself to the limit. Besides the physical challenge, I seem to be always trying to convince others of my value. Both Ron and Fred were better educated, had family money and already had a start on their own businesses. I came to Vail after being discharged from the army with $5 cash in my pocket, an old car with half a tank of gas and a sleeping bag. I had to work hard to prove myself and, in the long run, I knew that even if I did not win these boyish competitions, I had tried my best. That is something I have always been proud of."

I am touched by his honesty and straight-forwardness. "Lou, whatever happened to that bike?"

"I sold it at a garage sale for $100 before I moved to St. John, US

Virgin Islands in 1990. A few months later I bought a wreck of a boat that barely survived Hurricane Hugo. After going through some rough times, I began to rebuild it, along with my life. It's funny, I just told you about my resources when I arrived in Vail in 1967 and I suddenly realize that when I arrived in St John, I was in the same financial shape as I was when I arrived in Vail twenty-three years earlier. My life on St. John was about work, building the boat and getting my life under control. When I would tell people I moved to St John to get away from alcohol and drugs, they would laugh and say I came to the absolute wrong place. I kept my focus and made it happen."

"How did you decide on St. John?"

"This was a dramatic time in my life. The sale of my taxi and shuttle company in Vail went sour when the buyer quit making payments and filed for bankruptcy protection. Overnight, I was also bankrupt. Moe, you might not even remember, but I stored the white box and a few other items in your garage in Vail and drove off to California to reinvent myself. I quickly found that no one was looking for a forty-four year old jack-of-all-trades."

This is where I come into the story and add some spice to his life as we heat up a friendship forged years earlier. Lou and I and my former husband were all part of the same adventurous crowd in Vail. In 1994

Lou sold his boat, the *Lui-Nu*, which he had spent fourteen months rebuilding. He met me in Europe for a two-week backdoor tour of our own making. It was winter in Spain and too cold for any bike traveling, so we rented a car and covered quite a bit of the country before it was time for me to return to my home in Vail. We said good-bye at the airport in Miami. Lou went to California to figure out how the next chapter of his life would play out.

A few weeks later, he came to visit my daughter, Ailish, and me in Vail. It did not take long for me to get caught up in the magic of a blossoming relationship. But I hadn't realized how our affair was affecting Ailish. Instead of being honest with myself and my daughter, I treated this new arrangement very casually. Before long, we settled into what turned out to be a stressful transition for all of us. I became frantic with anxiety because having a man in the house was not easy for my daughter; Lou was not accustomed to living with a teenager and I found myself caught in the middle of one confrontation after another. Lou occupied his days by rebuilding our decks and taking care of many necessary home improvements. When this was complete, he knew he needed to once again figure out where he belonged.

Lou realized that I was in no position to shift gears in my busy life and go off with him on an extended journey. I had too many responsibilities as a director/teacher of a preschool, an adjunct professor at Colorado Mountain College and, most of all, a single mom raising a teenage daughter.

In order to give my daughter some privacy when she came home from school each day, Lou headed off to the library to research bike riding through Europe. This had been a dream of his for a long time. Since he was turning fifty the next year and tensions on the home front continued to heat up, the time for this adventure was at hand.

It was 1995 and this was a time in his adult life that he was not tied down to a job, had no financial obligations and was in the midst of a rocky relationship, so there was nothing to hold him back. After all, he was just "passing through" Vail. He had the money from the sale of his boat, and he felt like a carefree kid eager to embark on an adventure.

The hours he spent at the library gave him time to read bike magazines, travel guides and photo journals and to pour over endless maps of the European continent. He needed to determine the best route; he knew the trip should take place by the beginning of fall when the summer tourist crowd had departed but before the weather began to change. He was discovering there were many European countries he wanted to visit, but he also knew the narrow roads in Italy, France and Germany did not present a bike-friendly atmosphere. His research pointed to the low countries of Holland, Belgium and Luxembourg. Lou reflected on the many conversations he had over the past years with others who had biked Europe. He realized their experiences were now irrelevant as time brought with it an influx of travelers to the Continent and he knew that this translated to more, larger and faster cars on the roads.

Most of the articles in magazines on bike travel through Europe described group tours that involved support vans and overnight B & B stays. These trips carried with them very hefty price tags. Lou was certain of one thing; this would be a solo trip. He needed time to reflect on his past and contemplate what forces might be influencing his plans for the future. This journey, taking place in the here and now, would give him time to move in slow motion and the freedom to stop and explore when and where he wanted. He longed for the adventure and peace of mind such a trip could provide. He was confident that things would fall in place along the way, but he needed to make a commitment, buy a plane ticket and say good-bye.

First, he had to find the perfect bike.

From past experience, he knew that the bike for him would have to be custom-built. This took him back to the library where he researched bicycles and their components. His first-hand research visiting local ski shops that were eagerly preparing to replace the skis with bikes turned out to be valuable. He wanted a hybrid or cross-bike with wider tires than his old racing bike, circa 1970, Aspen, Colorado.

He made friends with a couple of young guys at a small shop in Lionshead in the Lifthouse Lodge. Together they discussed what might be the best piece of equipment for Lou's needs and pocketbook. The boys had just unpacked a Jamison Coda frame that would be perfect. They worked with Lou to come up with the best gearing for travel on narrow, and possibly hilly European roads. The price tag of $850 was agreeable. If he had had an unlimited budget and was going for speed rather than for the experience of the journey, he would have had them build a thing of beauty, a bicycle with a titanium frame that was a blend of workmanship, style and performance; and, yes, it would have come with a price tag of $4,000. What he needed was a workhorse: a machine he could count on to carry him and his belongings for many miles through rugged terrain. After a few test runs around town, the deal was finalized. Lou would also need panniers and other touring gear he could purchase slowly over the summer.

Lou made some test rides back and forth over Vail Pass, then to Steamboat Springs, ninety-eight miles away and, finally, a two-and-a-half-day ride to Taos, New Mexico, where he met up with old friends David and Ginger who had moved there from Vail. This was the perfect opportunity for my friend, Ann, and me to embark on a road trip from Vail to Taos. As a newly-divorced, single woman, I was learning to spread my wings and gain confidence in myself and eager to test my skills. We joined Lou and his friends in Taos for a short vacation, and he returned to Vail with us.

The longer bike trip gave him a chance to test the new bike on the open road and over several mountain passes. He already knew what it was like to ride hard and slow to reach a summit; working through the gears while exhausting your legs and lungs. He knew what it felt like to have gravity thrust you into an effortless yet terrifying freefall. The reward for riding hard uphill was worth the joy of the downhill thrill. After each trip, he made minor adjustments to the bike and/or his touring gear. He added a handlebar shock absorbing system so the bumps in the road would not aggravate his arm joints. Lastly, the boys at the bike shop were able to come up with a more comfortable seat for long distance riding.

Some say that playing the stock market is an art; others say it is a game. Before Lou left California, he and his buddy had invested some of his boat earnings in stocks that were not paying off. The realization that he needed to conserve his cash hit hard. The extended European bike tour he had dreamed of for so long might be a bit much. He knew he had to come up with Plan B.

One night at dinner, a thick cloud of tension lay over the table as Lou and my daughter had a confrontation over some minor issue. In an uncharacteristically strong voice, Ailish told him that he was not welcome in our house. At that moment Lou decided this was just what he needed in order to take the leap and set off down the road. But in which direction would he head, now that Europe was out of the question? We talked it over that night and realized that neither of us knew where the relationship was heading. I recognized that my daughter was my priority and there would be time for us later if it was meant to be. Both Lou and I were feeling that unless he left, none of us would be able to figure out where we stood.

The next day Lou took out the United States atlas and his address book that had recently been updated. He was searching for a place, heavily steeped in natural beauty that he had not explored before, and where he had friends he could stop and visit along the way. Yes, he would head northwest out of Steamboat Springs and ride to Jackson Hole, Wyoming, in the Teton Mountains, then north to Yellowstone National Park for starters. Summer was drawing to a close and the winds of fall could bring with it some unfriendly weather, but this man was never one to take the easy way out. Lou was curiously optimistic as he assembled his gear for his departure.

TIME TO PACK FOR THE PACIFIC NORTHWEST

two

I sat on the bed silently watching as Lou opened the chest that had become his personal space when he moved into my house. Molly, my yellow Labrador retriever, sat beside me and licked my face. She seemed to know that Lou, who had become her constant companion these last few months while Ailish and I were busy with work and school, would be leaving soon. At first Lou tried to kick the tempo up and engaged in light-hearted talk as he pulled each item out of the drawer, but quickly settled into the tone that had been set by both Molly and me. He was fully aware which items of clothing would be set aside for the bike trip and which ones would be packed for storage in the depths of the garage below us. I had a feeling that this quiet moment would leave an indelible impression on my memory.

I stepped outside to help Ailish with her homework and when I returned I noticed everything was either neatly packed into his large, purple dive suitcase or systematically stacked on top of the dresser. He was sitting on the side of the bed making notes in his small, green striped journal that I had given him when he first began talking of a bike adventure. "What are you writing?" I inquired.

"I'm making notes of what items I will need to purchase to complete my wardrobe for the trip."

I wondered out loud, "How do you know exactly what to bring along? The space is so limited, and you will be gone for an indefinite length of time. I would never be able to make that decision on the first try."

"Being prepared is a Boy Scout motto, but as I matured beyond my scouting days, I learned after I made my first skydiving jump outside of Vail at the Eagle Airport that being prepared could mean life or death. One day a guy by the name of Gordie Cummings walked into the Slope, where I was working, and told me he wanted to start a skydiving club and he needed some help. He said he had heard about me and my history of putting on events and thought the Slope would be a perfect place to promote the idea. I took a minute to think about his proposal and the fact that I had always wanted to jump out of a plane to see if it would cure my fear of heights. I heard a strong, "*yes, let's do it,*" come from my gut and within two weeks I was making my first jump."

"Oh my goodness, I can't wait to hear more."

Lou continued to distract me with his story; "The day of the jump dawned clear and bright, and I was given some last minute instructions and told as soon as the chute opens, look up and make sure that no panels have blown out from the pressure of opening. Well, after exiting the plane I looked up and sure enough there was a hole in the canopy. The problem was that I never bothered to ask how big a hole warrants you to cut away and use your reserve. It took an alarming amount of time to realize that I was not falling much faster than the divers who preceded me or even the ones who jumped afterwards, so I settled down and rode it out, and finally touched the ground with only a slightly sprained ankle. Moe, that's when I really learned the true meaning of being prepared."

"I never realized that you had done any sky diving, Lou, and believe me I am very impressed, but back to packing for this upcoming bike adventure."

"First of all, my recent ride to Taos gave me a good idea of what I would need to take with me and past experience has always been a reliable gauge as well. I have been studying the weather patterns and trying to anticipate the elements I will be up against, including being stranded in the middle of nowhere in a blinding snowstorm. The clothes are only part of what I will need to include. I have to be prepared to change a flat tire and make minor repairs and adjustments and, remember, there is the danger of bears at this time of the year when you are camping in the wilderness."

"Speaking of bears, remember when Shmo, my neighbor across the street, left his door open after having a little too much to drink while watching the final game of the Stanley Cup playoff? You walked out of my house the next morning and saw a four-foot-tall brown bear headed up the driveway to his front door. A few minutes later his dog came running out with his tail between his legs. I was in the house with Molly, totally unaware of what you were up to."

"I waited for the bear to walk out of the house and meander away, and then walked in to see if Shmo was still alive. The place reeked of cigarette smoke and stale beer, and there was Shmo passed out on the couch, none the wiser to how close he was to being eaten for breakfast."

"Yes, Lou, we have had our share of bears here in the Vail neighborhoods," I added, "But sleeping in your little tent under the stars in their neighborhood is another story. How will you protect yourself?"

"I'm not planning on carrying much food with me, other than a power bar or two, since food is what draws the bears to campsites. I have a container of pepper spray that should work for possible, threatening intruders lurking around my tent. Moe, I think the best way to describe my packing strategy is that I went about it like a well-trained Boy Scout. You don't think I would head out without first-aid supplies, like plenty of pain relievers for a sore butt, or a snake-bite kit?"

"With that last comment, I will do my best to think good thoughts and pray that you will have only friendly visitors to your campsite."

When Lou was finally ready to pack his panniers, he wrote down each item and its location in the front of his journal. He let me know how important it was for him to be able to get directly to what he needed without unpacking. "Moe, if I make changes along the way, I will make corrections on the list. That is why I wrote it in pencil."

I peeked over his shoulder and saw that each item was listed in pencil on the first page of his journal.

LEFT REAR: sandals, belt, hat, cowboy boots, Levi's, wool shirt, long-sleeve green shirt. TOP: 2-warm long pants.

RIGHT REAR: underwear, knee-wrap, rain gear, 2-turtle necks, scarf, warm gray shirt, long underwear, pink shirt. TOP: thin pants, towel, flashlight and battery, note pad.

RIGHT FRONT: beige pants, Levi shirt, 2-silk shirts, bathing suit. TOP: toothbrush stuff, battery, aloe spray, bungee cords.

LEFT FRONT: blue riding shirt, purple collar, red shirt, gray-T, black socks

HANDLEBAR BAG: power bars, drink mix, balloons, chain lube, battery, razors, bike computer, soap, pepper spray, gloves, camera, film and $ 3,000 in cash.

I carefully looked at the list and could see that the handlebar bag contained the items he would need at a moment's notice. I then began to smile as I questioned Lou, "I understand the wool shirts and the bathing suit, but why the cowboy boots and silk shirts?"

My Polish-American friend responded in rather a cocky way, "Because I am planning on visiting friends along the way in cowboy country, and I want to see the look on their faces when I come out of the guest room all spiffed up. I imagine they will still be in shock from watching me ride up to their house on a *bicycle*, and carrying cowboy boots in one of my packs will be the icing on the cake!"

THE LAUNCH:
BACK ON THE ROAD

three

The summer of 1995 was drawing to an end and the winds of winter may have been a bit too close for comfort, but there was no turning back now. We made a plan to have a private farewell party of our own in Steamboat Springs before Lou pedaled away on his journey. This time he would join me in the car and carry the bike along. Lou's spirit of excitement was contagious until the familiar Johnny Mathis song, *It's Not for Me to Say*, blasted from the CD-player. We refocused and promised ourselves that this would be an upbeat weekend and we would concentrate on the present for it was all we could count on for now. The skies were fading from the intense cobalt color to a soft shade of blue with a few puffy clouds in the distance.

As we drove to our favorite romantic B & B, I heard Lou's familiar laugh as he began to reminisce about his first bike ride and our overnight stay in Steamboat. "Moe, remember my first ride here when I called you at work and told you to get a move on? I had arrived at the Inn ahead of schedule and as we spoke I was sitting in the Jacuzzi waiting for you to arrive. I was also waiting for the innkeeper to return so I could check into our room, but what I didn't know then was that I was at the wrong B & B. When the innkeeper finally showed up, she gently informed me that I did not have reservations at the Steamboat B & B, but she would gladly place a call to the other B & B with a similar name. When she did, sure enough we had reservations there for the night. I thanked her and asked directions before calling you back in Vail. The disappointing thing was that I had already made myself comfortable and now I would need to dry off, get dressed and hop back on the bike for a grueling ride up to the ski area under a threatening black sky accompanied by a drum roll of thunder. By that time you were on the road to Steamboat and we reached the ski area at the top of the hill within an hour of each other."

I chuckled along with him, and said. "That was then and this is now. Tonight we have reservations at the most romantic spot in Steamboat Springs and you know the Jacuzzi well." We checked in, and drove over to the Yacht Club restaurant to have a delicious tuna capriccio and a glass of white wine at a beautiful table beside the gently flowing river. The sounds of the concert in the park drew us in before heading back to the B & B, where we topped off the evening with a soak in the Jacuzzi under the stars.

At breakfast, Lou did not hold back as he reached for one more piece of homemade bread, along with some tasty fruit and plenty of eggs and potatoes. He would need all the carbohydrates he could get to sustain him on the ride that lay ahead of him today.

We were both aware of the magnificent day that presented itself. Lou was especially anxious to proceed to Steamboat Lake to begin the adventure. When Lou was taking the bike out of the car and making the last minute adjustments to his gear, I stepped back, smelled the sweet morning air and watched as layers of light sifted down through the aspen trees around us. I noticed as he put on one and then the other well-worn sneaker that he didn't even have those fancy bike shoes that make the job of pedaling much more efficient. At least he had purchased a new pair of padded bike shorts. I agreed with him that they were more important than the fancy shirts with lots of pockets and the sleek shoes. Lou informed me later when I mentioned this to him that he carefully thought through the shoe issue and realized that biking was only part of what his trip would entail. He would need a shoe that would also work for walking and hiking and with limited space he did not want to carry more than the bare necessities except for, of course, the cowboy boots!

We didn't need to say any more to each other as our hearts were filled with mixed emotions and I knew the last thing Lou needed was to see tears rolling down my cheeks. I know my eyes must have been clouded with tears and my mind filled with visions of the past as well as a looming emptiness that would need to be filled in the days ahead of me. On my drive back I forgot to turn toward Vail and before I knew it I was driving east over Rabbit Ears Pass, heading in the wrong direction. At that moment I didn't care and, knowing that my daughter was away for the weekend, I was not in a hurry to return to my empty house. This was as good a time as any to explore a new area of Colorado. When I was back on I-70 and headed toward Vail, I decided that I would drown my sorrows by shopping at the Outlet Stores along the way. My favorite season for exploring the backcountry was just beginning and I was in desperate need of a new pair of hiking boots. With my purchase, I headed home. I simply went back to work on my life.

Molly, my faithful Lab, and her buddy, Zoie, greeted me as I drove into my driveway. This was just what I needed to resume my composure and tackle the days ahead. It was impossible not to love the furry pair for their beauty, exuberance and the undying devotion I would be in need of.

The days came and went as I waited anxiously to receive each animated phone call and letter that recounted every detail of Lou's life-changing adventure. I affectionately placed these letters; along with the notes I made after our phone calls and the photos I received by mail in a special folder.

At the same time, Lou was keeping detailed descriptions of each day in his small striped journal. Little did either of us know at the time that one day I would be transcribing these notes into a memoir of our life together.

It seems only natural that the following part of the book shifts gears and is written in Lou's voice as he describes not only the sights he is experiencing as he pedals west on his Jamison Coda, but also his most inner thoughts as he searches for direction in his future and clarity from his past that just might be buried in the stories he tells.

After we part and Moe heads home to Vail, I press on. Back on the unpaved road above Steamboat Lake, I am struggling with my squirrelly bike while realizing that the seventy-eight pounds I am carrying is not that well distributed after all. I stop to make a few adjustments along the way and discover that Moe has driven off with my air pump. The feeling of excitement turns to loneliness and fear as I think of flat tires, flash flooding, snakes and my tent being blown away in a deserted camping site. I know I have to focus on the road, and instantly take my mind back to the present. I could not have felt more blessed to be surrounded with breathtaking scenes in every direction.

This stretch of hilly road winds through aspen and pine groves with a brilliant blue sky overhead. The air is crisp and warming up quickly. I settle into my seat and realize I am living my dream! I pass several fantastic ranches that probably encompassed thousands of acres each. The gigantic log homes and out buildings are magnified by the endless expanse of green.

Within another thirty miles the scenery begins to change to flat, barren plains with a ribbon of asphalt under the bicycle. Not only does the scenery change, but the afternoon winds start to kick up and present a headwind that causes the euphoria to fade into grimace and pain. The sky grows pale and heavy while I am forced to stop and walk off some severe leg cramps. This would have been a great time to be part of an organized bike tour with someone following in a van carrying a handy massage table, but I had chosen to travel alone.

Several carloads of people stop along the way to say hi and ask where this tired, yet healthy-looking, middle-aged man is going on a bicycle in the middle of nowhere. Smiling broadly, I sense a hint of jealousy in their voices which gives me a boost in spirit and the energy to continue pedaling. Their interest and caring words make me feel like

I am either an oddity or a famous person. I laugh to myself and am pleased that I have packed my cowboy boots since I have an image to live up to. On the horizon, I spot a store where I stop for water and a candy bar. I approach the craggy old proprietor for advice and he lets me know I am only seven miles from Baggs, Wyoming, where I had imagined I might be spending my first night on the road in a cheap motel.

I settle back on my bike and ride into some strong winds. It doesn't take long to discover that with these fierce winds and the extra weight and width of the panniers hanging from each rear wheel. I will have to use the lowest gears available. I am being pushed around more than I feel comfortable with, but there is nowhere to go but straight ahead. Baggs has not changed from my earlier passage more than twenty years before, but this time instead of heading to a ski camp in the Tetons with a group of crazy thirty-year-olds, I am almost fifty and am pedaling solo. Since I have traveled a little over fifty miles today and it was pushing three in the afternoon, I decide it is time to stop for a good meal at a local diner and contemplate what might lie ahead for the rest of my first day. Striking up a conversation with a weathered local is easy and it convinces me that I will press on to places unknown rather than take that dumpy room in a little motel or, as the local suggested, sleep on a park bench.

I hop back on the bike and proceed on a flat road toward Creston, fifty miles away. The first ten miles are not too bad, but things get progressively worse. The swirling winds must now be forty–miles–an-hour and a looming storm that I knew I would be faced with is happening sooner, rather than later. I am even contemplating pulling over into a field and hunkering down in my tent for the night rather than being caught in the storm that was brewing up ahead.

A new model green van passes at high speed. The combination of the wind and the van passing almost blows me off the road. The couple in the car notices the weather conditions and the grimace on my face. They pull over and wait about a quarter of a mile up the road. They can tell this adventurer is not where he wants to be. The man shouts as I approach, "Hey, it looks like some weather is coming in and you could use a ride."

I stop, thank them profusely and ponder my options. Yes, my ego comes into this decision-making moment, but since this trip is about the journey and not a race, I remove the panniers, brake down my bike and hop in the back seat. I have been a loner all my life. I need to start to make an effort to expand friendships and dialog with other travelers. I recall that this is to be a solo trip, a time to search my inner spirit for my true essence, but I also know that my growth as a person can only be tested by being with others.

Robert and Elisa have been vacationing in the Vail area for the last week and are continuing their two-week trip, without their kids, in the national parks north of us. They seem pleased to have a new person to share stories with. I do not let them down. I tell them every old *Vail Tale* I can think of. I am more than ecstatic when I look out the window and realize I will be in an enclosed vehicle while passing this barren, miserable wasteland. I do not want them to drop me off before we get to Jackson Hole. We arrive there by 11 p.m., and I check into the Super 8 Motel for a good night's sleep.

Saturday, August 28, 1994, I wake up in God's country. I look around my room for a phone and contemplate calling Moe, but decide it is way too early; besides she would never believe I am already in Jackson Hole. I shower and prepare for the day by singing a medley of my favorite tunes with the unselfconsciousness of someone who thinks he is quite alone. It is still early and I do not want to pass up the opportunity to cruise the village of Jackson Hole without all my travel bags in tow. I choose what appears to be a local hangout for the older breakfast crowd and join a *cowboy* who is sitting alone at one of the bare-topped rustic tables. We share a few tales from our past and present and he fills me with advice about the road ahead. Before going back to the motel, I purchase an air pump, and thank God that I have made it here without a flat tire.

There isn't much to pack up at the hotel, so I proceed to give the bike a quick once-over and tighten a few bolts, put the air pump in its holder, refill the water bottles and climb on for the day's short ride to Grand Teton National Park. I decide I can wait no longer to call Moe to tell her about my first day on the road. She cannot believe I am already in Jackson Hole, Wyoming. Moe shares my excitement and I can barely detect a hint of sadness in her voice. Maybe this is a good move for us as a couple to separate and see what will present itself at the end of the journey.

The park road leads me along the base of the Teton Mountain Range and past Jenny Lake toward Jackson Lake. I recall that the cowboy at the local diner in Jackson Hole told me that a French trapper, who first discovered this magnificent range, called it *Les Trois Tetons* (the three breasts), as the mountains reminded him of a female body. I am not sure I am seeing the same vision, but do realize that these steep mountains that span forty miles in length and rise more than a mile above the valley of Jackson Hole were once rubble piles left by ice age alpine glaciers. Today the twelve peaks in the distance stand above the 12,000-foot level, and the range supports a dozen mountain glaciers. I suddenly feel small and quite humble.

These craggy peaks above me are ominous and seem to climb to the clouds then flow into the lakes below. My mind wanders a bit as I recall skiing in this wondrous area over twenty years ago. The ski area at Jackson Hole was much more rugged than the mountains I had learned to ski in Vail. Here, there were jagged cliffs and ravines that invited you to jump into their uncertain chambers. Perhaps this was the birthplace of X-treme skiing. In Vail, the upper reaches on the front of the mountain were gently sloping, while the back bowls offered some rim runs that were challenging in themselves. I recall that skiing in the Tetons offered an adrenalin-producing experience.

Before long, my imagination takes me back to a competition at the Jackson Hole Ski Camp with my old buddy, Ron Riley. We are racing against the clock; I am dressed in full padded racing gear, including a colorful gray and red sweater and snug fitting pants. I have strapped on my Soloman slalom-204 skis and am at ease in the moment. I am not feeling competitive, but instead am enjoying the experience and the warm spring weather. The gates are set up on a course that is quite challenging because of the pitch of the slope and the fact that, if you veered off course, you could end up in a header with a solid piece of granite. The varied spring skiing conditions — crusty and dangerous at 8:30 a.m. and slushy and dangerous by 10:30 a.m.— add to the treacherousness. Today I realize I am also at ease in the moment and am riding my bicycle for enjoyment.

I remind myself again that I am on a journey, not a race. I am carrying seventy-eight pounds of extra weight on my light-frame Jamison Coda. The sign for the campground appears around the next bend. I take the road and begin the search for a great campsite. I am pleased that it is only three in the afternoon. I have many choices at this time of the day. This will be the first time I am assembling my two-person, low profile tent. It takes only minutes and I am grinning as I look at the vista of Jackson Lake directly in front of my door and the dark clouds that are gathering above the water. Within minutes, the sky opens up and I settle into my small, snug quarters and listen to the thunder crashing overhead and behold and admire a lightening show directly in front of me. Let it rain! The timing couldn't have been more synchronistic. I am in no hurry as I wait out the storm. An hour later it has passed and I emerge from my tent to take in the fresh smell that surrounds me. I notice that there are three brilliant rainbows in the sky above.

Later that night, as I lay in my sleeping bag, I peer at the clear sky filled with stars and imagine that the stars are shining fish. The constellations become schools of fish being caught and pulled together in the nets of celestial fishermen. Why am I thinking about the ocean while I am in the middle of the Rocky Mountains? Is this a distraction for what might really be looming outside in the distance? Many thoughts come and go, but not for long as my tired body gives in to the battle against the mind to find peace for my first night in the wilderness.

I open my eyes and see the clear blue sky overhead and realize I have found my style: the previous day's ride, the glorious surroundings, my cozy tent, the crisp fall weather and my bike leaning next to the tree nearby. The dramatic sense of realism strikes me when I crawl out of bed. I am greeted by the cool morning air. I am anxious to see all there is in this park to which I refer as my hotel for the night. I tell myself that, just because I am on my bike, I will not miss any of the scenic sights, no matter how far I might have to detour to get to them and I will take pictures of everything to share with Moe. If these turnoffs from the main drag lead me to an unfavorable campsite tonight, oh well, it can't be perfect every night.

By 9:15 a.m. I have changed to short pants and a light jacket, but I notice in the distance that the weather is changing. I see that the grasses all around me have turned from the green of summer to a golden shade which will outlast the changing of the aspen trees which has not begun yet. There are no remnants of wildflowers, but I can imagine their brilliance only one month ago. Clouds are gathering and beginning to move in from the north. My plan today is to reach Bridger Campground in Yellowstone National Park. It is only thirty-four miles to the park's entrance and another forty-five miles to the campground. I feel like I am a part of the Greater Yellowstone Ecosystem, traveling like the animals between Great Teton and Yellowstone National Parks with seamless ease.

I ponder how this vast expanse of land (2.2 million acres) became part of the National Park system. I know that it is the world's oldest national park and that Yellowstone Lake is the largest high elevation lake in the western hemisphere. I stop at one of the scenic overlooks and read that I am biking on part of the 350-mile roadway system that traverses the park. The park's fauna includes wolf, coyote, elk, grizzly and black bear, bison, moose and pronghorn and bighorn sheep. I am sure that I will see my share of animals from the seat of my bike and my photos will be as close as one can get. Sure enough, while pedaling down the well-maintained park road, I spot an eight-point buck that has overtaken me and is now crossing the road in my path. I reach for my camera just in time as he lopes off into the green expanse below. I am saddened as I pass seared pine trees, a visual reminder of the great forest fire of 1988 which destroyed a lot of the southern part of Yellowstone National Park.

The ranger at the park entrance gate warns me about the approaching narrow road and the wider-than-wide RV's that take over the park during the summer months. I am in luck today as these vehicles are almost nonexistent. The first ten miles of this trail is uphill until I reach the summit at the Continental Divide. The river at the base of a deep gorge resembles a shiny piece of satin ribbon. It is not surprising that this, too, presents another photo-op.

Once the road drops down and levels off a bit, I am treated to a gentle stretch of riding with easy ups and downs. Perched upon the best possible viewing platform, I slowly pedal my bicycle toward the canyon floor. I am feeling very strong today and have been challenging the hills in higher gears. I am having no problem with leg cramping, but my butt will need three aspirins by the time I reach the campground. I decide to push on another twenty miles to the Bridger Campground even though the winds are picking up and the sky above has turned to an eerie shade of charcoal gray.

I am bordering Yellowstone Lake all the way to the campgrounds and, from time to time, I spot a large structure in the distance which looks intriguing. The surrounding pine forests, similar to those in Lake Tahoe, California, are bringing thoughts of my days there back to the forefront of my memory. It is spring of 1968, following my first winter in Vail. My buddy, Brian Woodel, invites me to join him before he takes off for a stint in the army. I want to explore the possibilities of living near this ski area as I have not made a commitment yet to return to Vail. My life is open for the next opportunity, but first I have to find a way to ski the mountain. I have fallen in love with the sport of skiing and know I want to live in a ski area where I can perfect the skills I have gained this year. I know the price of a lift ticket is not in my travel budget so I make a plan for the next day. I awake at dawn and dress in my ski clothes, shoulder my skis and walk toward the mountain. I proceed to climb up the side of the hill through the trees, with my skis over my shoulder and two hours later I arrive at the mid-mountain point where lift tickets are no longer being checked. Unfortunately, after one run, my feet are so tired and sore from the hike uphill in ski boots that I have to take the lift down. I wonder if the pain I am experiencing today in my rear end has reminded me about another time when my body was also suffering. One thing for certain, there will be no chair lift to carry me down the mountain tomorrow morning.

A few cars up ahead are turning left and I realize that I have finally reached Bridger and it is only 4:15 p.m. I pay the $2 fee for a camping platform for the night and begin my search for the best spot for my tent. I am delighted to find out there is a marina with fifty or sixty slips near the campground. I hurriedly set up my tent, and strike out for a short walk to the lake to find out what type boats are docked for the night. I am in such a rush that I almost miss the two deer that have crossed the path in front of me. I discover that there are a few forty-foot fishing boats as well as a pleasure craft tied up. Unfortunately, the restaurant at the marina is closed for the season and I am told the nearest one

31

is three miles further up the road. I realize I will be riding back to the campground through bear country in the dark, but the traffic is minimal and I have a flashlight. Sounds like an adventure to me! Dusk is approaching as I pedal toward the lodge. I am greeted by a moose grazing twenty feet off the road when I turn into the property. Further along the path, I am stopped in my tracks when in front of me stands that huge wood building I spotted earlier today when I was riding around Jackson Lake. I was not expecting anything so grand in a national park. This historic site, built in 1890, is now used as a 150-room lodge with a 575-seat restaurant, along with a bar and lobby.

The dining room is modern looking, considering the age of the building, with its light colored, country-style furniture. The room echoes *class,* not *rustic*, with the dining tables covered in white tablecloths and adorned with candles. As I glance out on the front lawn from my table, I am startled to see a buffalo reclining at ease fifty feet away. This is why thousands of people travel into the wilderness each year to gaze at such magnificent sights. Tonight I am just glad the parking lot and roads are not packed with oversize RV's. I peek around to find only a handful of other people dining. The prime rib is tasty and the wine a bit pricey for my budget, but what the heck, I am celebrating a seventy-eight- mile, seven-hour ride that I made today in this mountainous region.

If I had another glass of wine, I would toast John D. Rockefeller, Jr. who in 1927 founded the Snake River Land Company so that he and others could buy land in the area, incognito and have it held in a trust until the National Park Service could administer it. This private land purchase eventually became part of the Grand Teton National Park in 1949.

When I return to the biker's campground, I notice I have no neighbors and I am feeling a bit isolated and extremely tired. Settling into my snug quarters with a sky full of stars is becoming easy and comfortable. I am only hoping that the bears living in the woods do not smell the prime rib on my breath and think I have a snack waiting inside for them. Not another thought crosses my mind as I drift off to sleep and do not awake until the morning dew is thick on my tent.

ADVENTURES IN BIG SKY COUNTRY

four

The temperatures dipped during the night and fall is definitely on the horizon as I wake up to a chilly thirty-five degrees. I hike around the area while I wait for the sun to dry off my tent so I can pack up and be on the road. This is one of those mornings that I wish I had a coffee pot and a hot brew to warm my hands. I think about the days ahead and know I still have a few more in Yellowstone Park. I am reminded that, if I were racing rather than touring, I would be only seeing the road in front of me and the riders in back. I linger on the thought about all I have seen on my journey in three short days since I left Colorado.

I think about the difference in what my journey has become and that of a stage race; a multi-day event in which racers ride a given route. The cyclists rest overnight and the next day follow another route. The distances, just like each day of my ride, vary, but in a stage race, bikers are timed for each part of the race. They also have support vehicles which follow the racers. I smile when I think that I am carrying a fairly heavy load and have no van to assist in my journey.

As I leave Yellowstone Lake behind, I follow a wide river which winds its way along the side of the road. At one point, the Hardy Rapids appear and I am excited to see that they are still running with a little force after a long summer with minimal rain. A shiny white motor home with colorful travel decals slides by and blows my hat off. When I stop to pick it up, I am treated to the sight of two buffalo grazing right in front of me. I reach for my camera and snap the last picture on the roll and the last roll in my pack.

It is 9 a.m., my toes are still cold and I have on all my warm riding gear. As I glance at the sky above, I notice it looks faded because of the brilliant sunlight and I know that it is only a matter of time until I am stripping down and filling my packs with some of this clothing. When I round the corner, I see something that looks like it is out of the movie *Star Wars*. A dozen or so mounds resembling giant ant hills are spewing hot water and my camera is out of film! I stop to investigate the area by hiking in and around the mud geyser's terraced hillside. There are only a few other visitors who are exploring in a trance-like manner. I am saddened that I don't have any film to capture this amazing feat of nature. I worry about what else I will see before I am able to purchase another roll; maybe I will be able to find a postcard of this site.

Around the next bend, I enter Hayden Valley and spot at least 400 buffalo roaming the open range that extends over the next five miles. Could it be that today I am presented with the most magnificent sight, so far? I ride on and, within minutes, the valley and river widen and start to close in. I am approaching the Grand Canyon of Yellowstone and can hear the thundering sound of Yellowstone Fall's 300-foot drop of cascading water in the distance. I turn off the main road and ride in three miles to Inspiration Point. I have been told that this is a *must-see stop* on anyone's trip. The towering falls leading into the canyon can be seen from all directions. I know I can't leave without my own images of this moment, so I glance around and can't miss the photographer who is setting up his tripod. I approach and ask if he will sell me a roll of film. He obliges without hesitation and continues with his technical adjustments. My timing is right as the light is perfect for some beautiful shots of the falls. Before leaving, I stop to chat with the park ranger stationed nearby. He lets me know that snow is forecasted for the high country tonight.

Maybe snow is predicted for later tonight, but at 11 a.m. the temperature warrants me stripping down to my bottom layer of light clothing. When I check my odometer I am not surprised that I have only traveled fifteen miles by lunchtime. I am eager to press on, but stop to ask several rangers which of my options offer the prettiest scenery. They all agree that Tower Falls over Dunraven Pass at 8,895 feet would offer the most magnificent views, but they take one look at my graying beard and say they would not recommend it for bikers. Well, not to be cocky, I am confident that an 8,895- foot pass would be an anthill compared to others I had climbed back in Colorado. I thank them, place my helmet on my head and proceed to climb the seven miles to the summit. Yes, I am right. The climb is not at all difficult, but the temperatures are decreasing as I travel up the mountain and I notice that fluffy, fast-moving clouds are not that high above me.

At the top, I put on my jacket and glance at the haze in the distance, looking toward Idaho. A late season forest fire is blazing in that area. I am mentally preparing for my descent, expecting to be flying downhill at thirty-miles-per-hour, but instead find the first mile consists of a mini-roller coaster ride that finally leads to that fast pace I have been looking forward to. I am whizzing down the mountain for my last ten miles to Tower Falls. I don't think about what would happen if my pannier rack broke or the thin strips of rubber holding me upright above the road were to pop. I most assuredly do not even think of reaching for my water bottle or grabbing my camera for a photo. I focus on the road in front of me as I clutch the handlebars and hold on tight. The parking lot for the falls appears without any warning signs. I have to slow down very quickly in order to make the turn into the lot. For the first time on the trip, I find a crowd. I am in a packed parking lot with nowhere to secure my bike so I make the decision to just relax on one of the gigantic boulders in the sun, enjoy a snack and make some notes in my journal from today's ride.

I think back about what the park ranger said and wish I could tell him how off-base he was to insinuate that a biker my age should not take the route over Dunraven Pass. As I head toward the last part of today's journey to Mammoth Hot Springs, I take a slow pace up the mountain for a short stint which allows me time to dwell on the majestic cliffs on either side of me. From time to time, I am able to hear and see that the shale is falling away from the sides of the mountain into the abyss below. The canyon narrows as I begin to pedal uphill and then down for three miles before it opens into a big valley. I am amazed as I ponder the fact, that in the last twelve miles I have descended about 2,800 feet. The terrain changes rapidly from high meadows and burnt forest to vast, rolling, golden hills.

Maybe I have spoken too soon as I leave the valley floor behind again and wind up repeating the ups and downs three or four times over the next nineteen miles. I still have the energy and desire to take one more side trip to see a petrified tree which turns out to be no more than a petrified stump. The people in the cars ahead of me don't even get out and take a closer look. I have about seven miles to go with the winds accelerating. The last hour riding into Mammoth brings excruciating pains across my shoulders and my buttocks. Once in Mammoth, I stop to check out the ice cream selection at a local market and, two scoops later, I am feeling better.

Before long, I stop at the Yellowstone Hotel and Cabins, built of wood and timbers during the 1890s and there, grazing on the lawn in front of me, is a herd of thirty or more young reindeer. I soon discover that the hundred hotel rooms and cabins are full for the night. It looks like I will be testing my tent and sleeping bag for comfort in the below thirty-degree weather forecasted for tonight.

I pedal off to the campground a mile away and set up my tent in a twenty-mile-an-hour wind. I tie on all the lines I have brought along to secure my tent before heading off to find directions to the hot springs. The ranger in the campground tells me the springs are only two miles down the road. He explains that I will need to leave my bike in the parking area and hike in for half a mile. Before riding off to the hot springs, I decide to check my tent one more time for security. I can't get my mind off my sore body parts and wonder if I can make the ride. At that moment, Tracy and Bob from Ann Arbor, Michigan, pull into the campground only two spots away from my tent. I hear their laughter and wander over to introduce myself. The couple is intrigued when they hear that I am traveling alone on a bicycle. They also want to go to the hot springs, but having dinner seems to be their priority. Tracy invites me to have dinner with them and suggests that we go together to the springs after we eat. I am beginning to notice that friendships happen quickly on the road.

A few minutes later we are sharing stories and preparing dinner together as Bob opens a bottle of wine. Making connections requires participation and I am pleased to be a part of their team. I take a little taste of the pork chops, potatoes, salad, biscuits and cantaloupe and realize that I am having dinner with a couple of gourmet cooks. Unfortunately, the winds pick up and the temperature drops as we start eating. This sudden change in weather forces us to hurry through the meal before the blustery wind carries it away.

I rush back to my tent and dress in a t-neck, wool shirt, jeans and winter gloves before heading over to the hot springs with my new friends. I feel privileged to be inside their van and not on my bike tonight. After parking, we follow a trail down to the river through some brush and approach the rustic area from above. The steamy spring flows out of the side of the hill and down into the river below. A rock wall has been built in the river to separate the hot springs from the cold stream that unavoidably filters in. We are the only ones left when the busload of hippies leave shortly after we arrive. It takes a few minutes for my body to adjust to the temperature outside and the mixture of the hot and cold water in the river. I discover that the waterfall acts as a natural masseuse and my aching shoulders are treated to finger-like pressure from the pounding water.

I know that I have become a good storyteller when the travelers I meet along the road become mesmerized and hint for more. Moe always loved my stories, but I thought that was just love. Sometimes I wonder if I am living someone else's life or if I am now looking at myself from a different dimension. Which ever it is, I like it!

Back in my tent, I am fading off to sleep as I recall that I have hit speeds today of thirty-five-miles-an-hour and overall have averaged twenty-six mph.

When I wake up at 6 a.m. on the last day of August, it is icy cold. I unzip my tent to get a better look and there is no doubt in my mind that summer is over, even though it did not snow last night as the rangers predicted. The fading colors of the grass and bushes have a pale appearance and yet there is no hint of yellow or red in the distant trees. I know I will soon be treated to this colorful spectacle if I linger in the high country another week. The heavy morning mist and gray sky have  inspired me to snuggle into my sleeping bag for a short nap.

When I awake again I feel that early morning energy I love and am excited to take out my maps and plot the route for today. I decide to ride to Gardner for breakfast after packing up my gear. By 7:30 a.m. I am dressed in a turtleneck, wool shirt, jacket, gloves, winter riding pants and a knit hat tucked under my bike helmet. This is the kind of weather you don't mind riding up-hill in, but instead I am headed down the mountain for the five-mile ride.

Entering Montana, I pass a sign that says: *45th parallel of latitude, halfway between the equator and North Pole.* I cannot resist pulling my camera out of the handlebar pack and snapping a photo. This seems like one of those places in the world that you pass by only once in your lifetime.

Gardner is not much of a town; in fact the two-block area is actually a support community for Yellowstone National Park. It has one of those greasy old diners inhabited by an odd assortment of weathered cowboys who welcome a friendly face and are eager to share a story and a piece of wisdom. I fit right in at the counter and enjoy a large stack of hotcakes with bacon and a cup of steaming coffee. One fellow, who had obviously spent many hours under the hot Montana sun, told me that I would have one pass to climb on the way to Bozeman via Livingston. He even let me know that the winds would be at my side or in my face much of the way. It is time to go; so I say good-bye and am on the road by 9 a.m. facing another day of uncertainty and discovery.

The two-lane highway out of Gardner with its wide shoulder provides easy riding. I begin to think about how each day on the road begins with a clean slate and so far has been endlessly fascinating. I recall that as a child I loved the unknown. I sometimes felt like I lived in a mysterious world when my parents and other elders around me spoke Polish, a language my siblings and I never understood. One day, when they were deep in adult conversation, I went up to the attic and hid. They soon discovered that I, the youngest, was nowhere to be found. They frantically searched the house for their precious little boy. I waited silently and savored how this display of attention made me feel loved. My brother even spotted me under a shelf in the attic and did not give away my hiding place. I don't recall if the outcome of my prank ended with hugs and kisses or some sort of punishment. I am strongly aware at this moment that your past impacts your future. I wonder if I am taking this trip partly to get attention and respect from someone, maybe Ailish, Moe's daughter, who wanted me to disappear from their life.

I bring my attention back to the road. I notice that the valley I am riding within stays narrow with the river running alongside. There is a peaceful feeling as I take in the rocky canyon and grassy bogs on either side of me floating effortlessly by. Unfortunately this euphoria does not last for long. Instead the winds pick up and I have flashbacks of Baggs, Wyoming. A part of me wishes that green van with its jovial passengers would cruise by and give me a lift.

The turn off on the old road to Chico Hot Springs pops up out of nowhere and I hesitantly take the turn. I was told that the resort at the springs is exclusive and very expensive, but it is not in my nature to allow a warning from a stranger to stop me from heading in this direction. I am drawn to the idea of an oasis of hot water to soak my cold and tired body and I proceed along the river. This is another one of those scenic spots that few people ever experience in this manner. I only encounter two cars on this gorgeous fifteen-mile stretch. I am feeling pensive as I approach the Chico Hot Springs compound along a road that substitutes as a runway for private planes flying celebrities in for a secluded getaway. Will I be able to afford a room for the night? If worse comes to worse, I know that Livingston is only twenty miles away and I can surely find a $25-a-night room there. Time to get off my bike and go inside to see what I will find.

Luck is on my side as I am told that a room with a shared bath is only $40 for the night. I strip my bike down, store my panniers in my room and head out for a look around. The quaint main lodge was built in the 1920s out of wood and finished with brick fireplaces and wood-plank floors along with plenty of glass to look out into Montana's big sky. I am aware that the building was once a sanitarium and, as I sit in the pasta restaurant enjoying my $8 pizza, it looks like some of the patients have come back to visit. I am told that the place rocks on the weekend, but for now, the crowd in the four or five rented rooms is far from the celebs I expected to find sitting next to me in the hot pool.

I am more than ready to dip my tired and sore body into the hot water for my first soak of the day. Alone in the hot pool, I savor the last strong rays of the sun and am glad that I am a guest in the hotel rather than a patient in the sanitarium of long ago. The hot water relaxes every muscle and makes it difficult to climb out of the pool, but I manage as I am eager to slide between the sheets on my antique bed perched in front of a window for an afternoon nap. Now this is luxury!

I am amazed at how easily I am able to slip into the rhythm of relaxation. I feel more like a tourist than a traveler today since I have covered only thirty-nine miles and have been in one spot most of the day enjoying the hotel's amenities. Travelers are on an extended tour and tourists are around for only a few days. Tourists tend to see the sights, eat in the best restaurants and soak in the pool: yes, that's me today! But as I think about it, I am missing the backpackers whom I meet in the national parks. They tend to be more relaxed, more frugal and are friendlier than the typical tourist. There are no age barriers and there is always someone ready to say, "Let me tell you a story."

As the day rolls on, the hotel begins to fill up. I even hear a small plane landing on the road leading to the hotel and ponder who might be arriving in a private plane. It is time for another soak in the pool before having dinner in one of the hotel restaurants. I know I will not be taking a table in the formal dining room with an a la carte menu starting at $20 a plate.

I am feeling a little lonely tonight, and head back to my room after dinner to make a few entries in my journal before falling off to sleep. Tomorrow I will be with my old Vail buddy, Ralph. I fade off to sleep thinking about the '60s when Ralph worked for me at the Slope Bar in Vail. Town ski races were very big business in those days and many of the bars and restaurants sponsored a team and, of course, the team and its following always partied at *their* watering hole. I was in charge of the races for Ski Club Vail and Ralph was one of the Club's coaches. He was also a great skier, the kind who could assure your team of top placement in the ranks. It seemed like a clever move to hire him to work in our bar and restaurant and reap the benefits of his special talents.

Ralph was a prototype of Black Bart with a big handlebar mustache, a muscular frame and rough mannerisms to round out the profile. He chewed tobacco and drank Jack Daniels straight from the bottle. Ralph felt that the longhaired hippies, who were ever present during the '60s, should be exterminated. On one snowy New Year's Eve, Ralph was scheduled, to his chagrin, to work in the bar cooking frozen pizzas if and when any were ordered. About ten that evening he stumbled out of the kitchen and it did not take long to see that he was three sheets to the wind. He spotted Graham, a local artist who happened to wear his hair long, sitting at the bar and sauntered over with at least three chips on his shoulder and started taunting him about being a *no-good hippie*.

This quickly escalated and Ralph threw a quicker-than-lightening right punch at Graham's face. I had no choice except to fire him that minute in spite of needing his help on the busiest night of the year and the fact that he was our ringer for the ski team. We somehow remained friends and he could have cared less about losing his job; in fact, he never wanted to be working on New Years Eve in the first place.

With the sun's earliest rays, I wander over for the breakfast buffet and allow myself the luxury of sampling a variety of egg dishes, crispy bacon, some tasty fruit and a piece of sugar-spattered French toast. I look around and see a few sleepy faces and hear little conversation taking place. I realize this breakfast will be a solitary moment as I sit alone in the dining room.

I assemble my bike and panniers and am impressed that I know every bit of it so intimately. In just one short week I can make adjustments in minutes. I am able to find every item without looking at my list when I need something. I seem to have included just the right items so far to make my trip comfortable. I glance at Montana's big sky and see that there is an assortment of fluffy clouds overhead, but today the temperature is much warmer than when I was riding at higher altitudes.

It is 8:30 a.m. and I am on the road riding toward Paradise Valley. I have no idea what I will find as this is a new part of the country for me and I had no bikers to confer with at Chico. The high peaks that were towering above me disappear and I seem to slide easily into miles of golden grasslands. This past twenty miles has been a great ride, much like the ride through Glenwood Canyon, in Colorado.

When the ride is effortless, I sometimes just sink into the euphoria of the moment and let the road take me along. At other times, I find myself reflecting on my past as if my bike seat were the couch in the psychiatrist's office and me the patient trying to unravel the meaning of my life. I have learned not to dwell on the future because it is so uncertain at this time. Instead of being afraid of this, I am letting it unfold with each bend in the road that I travel on. I am trying to look at myself from a different dimension.

I ride up the forty-eight easy miles to the top of Bozeman Pass. I have been waiting for another adrenaline ride just like this one that comes with the downhill at thirty-seven- miles-per-hour. I am treated to ten miles of that with my headphones on and Bob Dylan singing

Like a Rolling Stone blasting in my head. This is the song that gave me the inspiration to get out of Detroit and eventually directed me to Vail, Colorado.

As I approach Bozeman, another flashback of my early days in Vail as race chairman brings Ralph to the forefront of my thoughts. It is the National Veteran Ski Championships and I am chairperson for the week-long events. Being involved with the Vail Town Race Series and Vice President of the local ski club, I collaborated with Ron and Jim to convince Bill Brown, the head of mountain operations, to allow the local town downhill race to take place on the same course as the Vets race, starting the day after they vacated. Vail Associates did not want the locals to race on the Lionshead course because of the added expense for grooming and personnel. The town races had always taken place on Gold Peak, which was not challenging enough for this three-day downhill event. I was involved, as a competitor and an organizer, in both races and gave my word to Bill Brown that there would be no problems on the hill. He realized that using the course for both events would make economic sense because the course prep would already have been done for the Vet's event.

The setback started when I blew my knee out in the Vet's race and ended up in the hospital. I was unable to supervise the downhill event so I asked Ralph, who was one of our best coaches, to take over for me and co-ordinate things on the mountain. It seemed like a no-brainer until I got a phone call from Bill Brown himself who was fuming because Ralph had told a group of skiers (paying customers) on the hill to, "Get the fuck off the ski run. Can't you see there's a race going on?" Once again he was relieved of duties and, once again, he took it with a grain of salt and we remained friends. Politics was never his game.

I am chuckling as I pull into his bar, the Rocking R, at 12:30 p.m. and find out that Ralph is out grouse hunting and will return later in the afternoon. I feel the urge to leave, rather than wait around the bar. I take the opportunity to explore Bozeman on this beautiful, warm afternoon. I spot my favorite yogurt shop next to a Laundromat and have a double scoop before heading over to do my laundry and mail off a few rolls of film to Moe. Outside the shop I meet a couple who are biking down from Canada and we compare notes on the routes I am contemplating on taking in a few days. This is a synchronistic moment as I was hoping I would find someone in town who has had some experience with biking in this area who might give me a heads-up about the path north towards Canada.

MEETING THE PAST, FACING THE FUTURE

five

"Lou, my husband will be back any minute, why don't you just come on out to the house?" said Fay. "I have been hearing stories about you since Ralph first got the news of your visit. I want to meet this character from my husband's past who is traveling on a bike." She gives me the directions for the seven-mile ride up to Bridger Bowl and I let her know I will be arriving soon.

Fay had told me to follow the signs to the ski area just beyond their house along a two-lane paved road. I can feel the area closing in as I pedal past fields lined with gigantic golden hay bales and a few farmhouses and barns. I am surrounded by what we call foothills in Colorado. I reflect on the Town of Vail Downhill race many years ago when we felt like Golden Peak on Vail Mountain would not be fast enough for our caliber of racers. I imagine Ralph does not spend much time skiing in Montana with the size of the peaks in the distance, or does he quench his thirst for adrenaline somewhere else?

I pull into the driveway and ride toward a large white house with a high-pitched roof and a front porch supported by tall, stately columns. The ten-acre ranch seems to be bordered on the far side by tree-covered hills. There is an indoor stable, tack room and fenced area for horses on my right. Looks like the home of a proper cowboy. Fay comes out of the front door just as I pull up, and makes me feel welcome.

When she goes inside to answer the phone, I start to unpack my stuff and who drives up in his truck but Ralph. His loud voice resonates as he slaps me on the back and says, "Jesus Christ, you rode your bicycle up here from Colorado. I thought you were on a Harley or something."

"Yeah, Ralph," I respond, "I like the exercise and view I get from the seat of my bike and it is a lot quieter than a Harley. Well, I found your house and am only planning to stay a few months." He does not respond, so I let him know I am just kidding. "I do appreciate you sheltering me from the Labor Day weekend traffic on the highways through the mountains."

He barely gives me time to put my things inside the house before whisking me back to town. Not only is Ralph notorious as the owner of the most popular bar in Bozeman, but he is also a stock car racer and tomorrow night is the last point-race of the series.

He and I go over to his garage to do some work on his race car, and he hands me a card printed with a photo of himself dressed in a yellow jumpsuit and cap standing next to his late model bright yellow #5 race car in front of his Golden Goose Casino. The card says that Ralph has had eight years experience as a racer and is third in points for three years in a row. I realize that this is a bit more than a hobby, and know that my *amigo* has found another way to experience a thrill just as he did so often on the racecourses on Vail Mountain. Ralph introduces me to the mechanic as his crazy friend who rode his bicycle all the way from Colorado. The mechanic and other assistants are busy fine-tuning the machine and pay little attention to me until Ralph says that I will assist them on the pit crew tomorrow night. One of them passes me a yellow T-shirt with Ferraro Motor Sports printed across it and a cap they instruct me to wear for tomorrow's race. As we are walking out, the head mechanic tells me that my job will be to help change tires.

Within an hour we are heading back to his homestead. As I wander around the house, Ralph and his wife are discussing Ralph's plans for the weekend. This seems like a good time for me to take a shower and pull out my best duds for the evening ahead. This is my first chance to dress up in my western wear, including my cowboy boots, and see if I get the reaction I am looking for.

Sure enough, they respond instantly and ask how I could have had room in my bike packs to carry dress clothes, let alone keep a crease in the jeans. I proudly join Ralph and Fay in the kitchen and am handed a glass of red wine for the first toast of the night. Has Ralph matured and is no longer drinking Jack Daniels from the bottle, or is this just a slow start to a long evening? I am given the job to make the salad, while Fay and Ralph put the finishing touches on the lasagna and garlic bread.

After dinner Fay seems to disappear: in fact I saw little of her or the rest of the family during this entertainment packed weekend. I guess I bring the *machismo* out in my Italian friend, and we head off to his trophy room to shoot some pool and have a few more after-dinner drinks. Trophy Room is an understatement for this magnificent high-ceilinged room with leaded windows that looks out onto the expansive golden lawn and rolling hills in the distance. The walls are adorned with deer, elk, antelope, moose and mountain goat trophies, and a huge antler chandelier hangs over the leather couch and chairs. Not surprisingly, the room has a full-sized pool table and a big screen TV. This is definitely Ralph's room where he entertains his buddies long into the night.

The evening turns out to be a tantalizing mix of the old and new. As we talk I can just about see the conscious reshaping of our lives, and at that moment I observe that Moe has become a very significant agent of change in my life. I gather my composure and know that I will think more about this later. But for now; Ralph and I are a couple of kids trying to one-up each other with our tales of adventure until we run out of stories and know we need time to conjure up more for the next few days. We say good night and stumble off to our rooms.

Above the door of the guest room where I am sleeping, I notice a decorative plate with a picture of Princess Di, and this reminds me of the time that Princess Diana from the United Kingdom visited Vail. She made the mistake of visiting the ladies room at Uptown Grill Restaurant, and Packy Walker, being the observant bar customer, immediately entered the bathroom after her departure and removed the toilet seat. A few days later the toilet seat was mounted on the wall in another restaurant, Bart & Yeti's; with a plaque saying "Princess Di sat here." I can't help but chuckle as I drift off to sleep.

I awake with the first sounds of morning and walk outside into a landscape so bright I have to raise a hand to shield my eyes. It is clear why Montana is called Big Sky Country. There are no clouds overhead and the temperature is the warmest I have experienced in the last week. Before Ralph joins me, I have a chance to reflect on last night's conversation and am taken back again by the thought about Moe becoming such an important component in my changing life. I know I will have more time to ponder this in the long ride ahead of me, but for now, I am summoned to join Ralph on his daily errands around the town he has become an integral part of.

The Golden Goose Casino, his latest business venture, is our first stop. The place is not as elegant as the name and I can see that it is not much bigger than Ralph's trophy room. The casino has an assortment of slot machines, a few gaming tables and, of course, a bar and restaurant. I am sure I will gather a different impression when I see it later tonight filled with people deeply engaged in betting against the machines or one another. Ralph tells me that it is the gaming license, not the nightly take, which will someday assure him of a cushy retirement. My entrepreneurial soul is elated, and I admit that I am a tiny bit envious with all Ralph has accomplished since the early days when he was a ski bum in Vail.

The day has flown by and it is already 5 p.m. We are heading over to the garage for a pep talk with the crew and to check last minute tune-up preparations. I am impressed at how seriously the team works together. One thing I am not used to from traveling alone this last week is the constant companionship of others. I have mixed feelings, but none-the-less, I am energized and ready to jump in and become a part of the group.

Once we are in the race grounds, I am a bit overwhelmed by the crowd in the stands and the number of people and motor homes in the inner circle, or pit crew area, that is surrounded by a half- mile clay track. No doubts about it, these westerners know how to party; but for now, there is business to take care of. I change a few tires, do my share of hooting and hollering and am pleased that my old ski buddy has won two out of three of his events. We all head over to the Rocking R, owned by Ralph, to have a few beers or shots of Black Jack to celebrate a winning season at the racetrack.

I get a chance to see what makes the Rocking R the most rock'n place after midnight in Bozeman. It is a mix between Alice's Alley, a pool hall and beer joint that another good friend, Jon Boss, ran in Aspen, and Donovan's Copper Bar in Vail, which was frequented by the ski patrol, ski instructors and all locals and tourists. It is the kind of place where rules of etiquette do not exist. If someone wants to dance on the bar, roll the dice or make out in the corner, they can do it at the Rocking R. There are no age barriers with the customers. The Montana State University students mix with the cowboys and cowgirls of Bozeman, with all having the same goal in mind: to party hardy, deep into the night. I can barely recall getting back to Ralph's house, but know that sleep was a welcome relief to the day I experienced as Ralph's shadow.

The way I feel when I wake up the next morning tells me I am right in sync with the rest of the folks at the Rocking R. It is Saturday and I realize I have been traveling for only a week and what a week it had been! I know it sounds crazy, but I am actually looking forward to getting on the road again and exploring the back country to the north of Bozeman. I still have a few more days to spend with the Ferraro family, and I was never a slacker when it came to partying, so I better get a move on.

Today is the day of the big Montana State football game against one of their rivals, whose name I did not remember after the cheering. Ralph is a big fan of Montana State, not because it was his *alma mater*, but because the students are a big part of the customer base at his bar and restaurants. We leave the house by 9 a.m. and pick up the motor home, and stock it with food, ice and beverages at the restaurant before heading to the stadium.

Finding the best strategic location to park for the after-game tailgate party is Ralph's objective when he pulls into the stadium lot. Ralph and I saunter over to the stadium entrance while stopping to talk to many people along the way. It seems difficult for Ralph to pass a fellow football fan without sharing a word or two.

A war of colors rages from the stands that are packed with students, alumni and their guests; and on the field with the two opposing teams, cheerleaders and marching bands. Since Ralph is an alumni supporter, he has tickets to the hospitality tent, and as I recall, we spent more time there than in the stands that entire day.

The 37-7 victory is cause to celebrate with a continuous tailgate party in the parking lot until the sun goes down. Rockin' out in the trailer reminded me of the time I borrowed a motor home from a friend in Aspen, and drove over to Vail to pick up Packy Walker and the Garton brothers, along with a girlfriend or two of theirs. We started the day with mushroom julips to get us prepared for the drive to Fort Collins for a Rolling Stones concert. It took us about ten hours to drive the usual four-hour journey. As the years passed my memories of the road trip and concert have faded and what is left is way too scary to dig deeper into. I have a feeling that the days ahead just might rival this experience, but on second thought, I am not at the wheel of the RV this time, and I am confident my buddy and I are much smarter than I was back in the '70s. This night, for us, is only beginning as we make our way over to the Rocking R where Ralph introduces me to the coach of Montana State and other notables that are there to celebrate the beginning of the football season with its first victory.

Later that night, I notice several cowboys at the bar playing an interesting dice game they call Bankers Dice, and before long they invite me to join them. A few hours later I am $650 richer. Luckily, Ralph is ready to leave and call it a night before my winnings are in someone else's pocket.

The next morning, I help Ralph corral two horses, as he is taking his daughter riding today. I am exhausted and welcome a day to myself. I take advantage of Fay's offer to use the laundry facilities; and in between loads, I relax on the couch and watch football. I doze off thinking about how my old ski buddy's life has changed since our days together in Vail. I reflect on his ten-acre ranch, five horses, three dogs, one mule, one wife, two children and a cat.

When I wake from my nap, I check my bike from head to tail and plot my course for tomorrow's ride. This is an unusual day for me on my bike trip, but I sink into the uneventfulness of it and wait for Ralph to return and reciprocate for their hospitality by taking him and his wife to eat steak and lobster at Logan's, a popular Bozeman restaurant.

HEADING FOR
THE FAR NORTH

six

I feel certain with each breath of clean, cool air I breathe that I am not running away from anything, but toward adventure. I am anxious to pedal to places unknown. My panniers are packed, my bike is adjusted and I settle into what will turn out to be a 114-mile ride today.

While pedaling off down the country road, I have a flashback and wonder if it is a dream I had last night. I am a kid, fourteen years old, and I'm riding alone on a bus into downtown Detroit. I get off the bus and start walking around in what appears to be a very unsafe neighborhood. Could this be just an image of how anxious I was to expand my world even at age fourteen? My flashback does not end here; it goes on to include a scenario that happened a few years later. My dad found maps in my bedroom with a route marked from our house in Michigan to Florida. Fearing that I might run away from home, he pulled me aside for a long scolding discussion that ended my plans to leave in the morning. I drift back to reality and make a mental note to call my Dad today and let him know I am ok.

At 8 a.m. I head west on the Frontage Road for thirty miles to Three Forks, where I stop at Sacajawea's Inn and Restaurant for breakfast. I like having the opportunity to dine in a historical site when the opportunity presents itself.

Sacajawea's was built in 1910 and refurbished to its new splendor in 1991. It is a four-story, red brick and stone Victorian with a hint of *hippie*. The upper two levels of the front of the building, where the guest rooms are located, are decorated with inlaid wood rainbows and floral design. The stained glass on the front door is ablaze with color as I enter and find a table by the window. I linger over breakfast and explore the well-groomed gardens and Inn before heading back on the road.

Gold is the color that is most evident when I look around these last few days. I had expected to encounter the reds, yellows and greens as well, but so far the leaves have either changed in the high country or not yet made the transition at the lower altitudes. I do not know what tomorrow will bring. I just take in the golden glow of the hay and wheat fields as the valley widens and I head toward the mountains.

Temperatures have risen from thirty-eight degrees when I started out this morning to seventy or so by noon. I am ready to shed my shirt for the first time and catch a few rays on my back as I pedal on. There is no wind, and not a single white fluffy cloud floats above me. It is truly a glorious day.

The headwaters of the Missouri River pop up on my right and I pedal alongside for a while. The river crisscrosses the highway and the mountains are on my right. Train tracks line up on my left and I think nothing of it at first, then when I hear the roar of an engine behind me, I imagine I am being approached by a semi, but when I glance into my side mirror, there are no trucks on the road. The noise gets louder and seems to be bearing down on me and yet I see nothing. It is a bit unsettling until I finally catch a glimpse of a train from the corner of my eye. The trains pass on an hourly basis and I take comfort in knowing they are on a track and not on the road, pressing down on me.

I am lost in the glare of the sun as I approach a recreational area along the river. This snake-like body of water that has been playing crisscross with me for the last few hours has widened and taken on the appearance of a rippling lake. I am stunned to see water skiers, motor homes, and campgrounds all around. The area is called Canyon Ferry Lake. I pass my first *for sale* sign since I left Bozeman. I get a feeling that the people in this area of the country are not eager for development to take place. I know that if this were Colorado, there would be a golf course, ski area or resort somewhere up here in God's country.

The road for twenty miles bordering the lake has become very narrow and the shoulder has been grooved to keep drivers from dozing off to sleep. This may be good for them, but it is playing havoc with my Jamison Coda and making it a squirrelly ride for me. I have to resort to a test of skills by trying to stay on the white line and off the shoulder bumps. I attack it with courageous exuberance and, before long, the shoulder returns to a full riding lane and I cruise into Helena.

I ride around town, find a frozen yogurt shop for my afternoon *cocktail* and ask about the camping options in the area. I am directed toward the KOA campground that has a pool, hot tub, showers and a movie showing tonight - all for only $14.60. I locate a restful spot, and set my tent up in a grassy area under a tree beside a picnic table with only the sound of squirrels running up and down the trees to distract me. I have found that even though I am not eating at my campsite, the picnic table comes in handy for propping up my bicycle and for packing and unpacking my stuff.

The night is long and cold and I awake with frost on my tent. Instead of snuggling back into my down sleeping bag until it warms up, I hop out and dress with all of my warm weather gear, including winter hat, jacket and gloves. I go over to the bathrooms to use the hand blower on my fingers that are frozen from packing up my gear. I need a cup of coffee and the manager invites me into the office to share a brew and warm up. He explains that this KOA campground is in a valley below town and some type of inversion causes it to be cooler than the surrounding areas. This is good news and encourages me to ride to a higher altitude as quickly as possible.

Within two miles, I am already stripping down to shorts, short-sleeve shirt and light wind-breaker. My plan is to have breakfast, fill up my water bottles and check my maps at the last restaurant on the way out of town. Before I know it, I have passed the last restaurant a few miles back and am heading up McDonald Pass with an elevation of 6,320 feet. I decide to continue, thinking something will pop up on the road ahead. It is only a 2,200-foot elevation increase, but to my surprise, I groan as I look up a huge incline. The road continues going uphill for over twenty miles and it feels a bit like riding over Vail pass following a night of too much partying.

I know I can reverse this slump I am in when I look around and realize that the scenery is gorgeous. The road is wide, the temperature perfect for bike riding and I have about four ounces of water left in my bottle and a power bar so I just kept turning the wheels and three hours later, I am at the top of the Continental Divide.

Even though my stomach is grumbling and I am extremely thirsty, I am going to stop and take in this glorious view from the summit. I reflect on my short history of parachuting from a plane into the Rocky Mountains and wonder if I would ever have the courage to do that again. But for now, I have the gift I have been waiting for on the horizon. Riding downhill, I slip my feet into my clips and attack the hill with gusto.

These positive thoughts turn into a bit of good luck as I spot a natural spring in the mountain side. I stop to quench my thirst and fill my water bottles. This will sustain me for a couple more hours until I find an open restaurant. I need to loose a little weight and a day like this will only help my personal goal.

A diner pops up along the side of the road, and I am beaming to see the faded sign out front. I bring the maps into the roadside diner and stretch them out on a table while I am waiting for my meal. I need to make a decision as to whether to head into Missoula on a bit of a treacherous highway to visit an old acquaintance or proceed toward Sealy Campground. I try Munsie's phone number, but am unable to reach him. I remember that he has a wife and three children now and may not want to recall old stories of his single days in Vail. I let the vision of him wrapped in aluminum foil at a bachelor party fade from my memory as I savor my meal of pork chops and mashed potatoes.

North it is! I know I cannot make it to the campground by dark, but what the heck, I have a tent that I can pitch anywhere, and the weather is gorgeous - not to mention the vistas that surround me. The road, reminiscent of what I rode in Yellowstone, takes me up and down a series of rolling hills. Fifty miles into the day and my butt is already sore. A tiny negative thought creeps into my mind that maybe I made the wrong choice, but there is no wind and the ribbon of asphalt keeps unrolling in front of me.

I guess I spoke too soon. The wind now changes with every bend in the road and my water supply is getting low. I have come to recognize this as another three-aspirin day. At last I pedal into the foothills and turn north-northwest where I can see the snow-capped mountains of Glacier National Park looming in the distance. I welcome the sight of the river accompanying me on my left and the shoulder of the road is very wide. I see the town of Ovando in the distance and visualize my name on a tall, frosty coke along with plenty of fresh water to refill my bottles.

The cashier in the diner tells me there is a campground only eight miles up, just off the highway on the river. This has inspired me to sprint to my destination. The spot is dazzling and only four other campers are in the park. As quickly as I can manage, I assemble my tent in time to watch the sun go down over the mountains while tucked inside my sleeping bag. Before long, the moon surfaces and softly lights up my world. Minutes later, my eyelids close and I settle into darkness for some much needed rest after this mountainous eighty-seven-mile journey.

It is already the seventh of September, but instead of getting colder it seems to be warming up. Each morning I have some free time while I am waiting for my tent to dry out. I use it to record notes in my journal, check my maps and meditate on the day ahead. I saddle up and proceed toward the nearest breakfast restaurant, only four miles up on the road to Sealy Lake.

I remind myself that I am determined to savor each and every minute of my journey. I call my friend Blu Funk who lives in Big Fork, Montana. He is excited that I am on my way to visit him. It has been years since I have seen Blu. I recall that he is a bit younger than I, and he hung out with a hippie crowd that was not afraid to ski the steepest tree-covered slopes Vail had to offer. Blu owned several popular restaurants during his time in Vail. I am anxious to see his new establishment, Showthyme, in Big Fork. He tells me he has a busy schedule today and won't have much spare time, but tomorrow he will be free to show me around. I tell him I will see him *mañana*.

For today, I am riding through tall, massive pines on a road less traveled. The green grass is turning to a brilliant shade of amber; the dying plants have a hint of reddish color. There are glimpses of forested mountains around each bend. I am surprised when I pedal over a hill and see the first of several lakes directly in front of me. The lakes are dotted with wooden structures on small islands in the center. Salmon Lake has a very modern stone-and-wood Catholic retreat perched at the edge of the lake among a cluster of pines. I stop to take a photo to send to my Dad and immediately have a quick flashback from my youth of sunny summer days spent around and on the lake near my parents: soon-to-be-retirement house in Michigan. I learned a lot about building in those early days. Dad bought a lot and had a contractor build the outside walls and roof of the house. I, my brother Jim and a few friends from the neighborhood became weekend plumbers, electricians, insulation installers, drywallers - you name it. If there was something we needed to know how to do, we learned it from each other. For me, this learning experience has been beneficial to this day.

I can't help but notice the influence the lumber industry has in this area. There are several large mills and log home builders along the road toward Seeley Lake. I am astonished to see signs on fences in support of logging. I notice that because of the speed and number of timber trucks traveling the road. There are far more dead deer, skunk and squirrel than live ones. I shade my eyes and look down the corridor. I am surprised to see the landscape fill up with a well-maintained golf course and a Four Seasons Resort, built near a little village with small rustic summer cottages.

I make a stop at Isla Lake to take a break, make some notes in my journal and savor a power bar before taking my place again atop those two spinning wheels. As I place my feet into my clips, I realize that I haven't seen the snow-capped mountains today. Just as I pedal around the first corner, up pop the granite peaks over Summit Lake. The pines start to open up now and mountain ranges are on both sides of me. The pedaling seems easy and no matter how much I try to stretch the day out, I am traveling too fast.

I arrive at Swan Lake at 4 p.m. and find that the campground is across the street from the lake and sits in the thick pines. I really wanted beachfront again tonight! I decide to drive up the road looking for another campground. The signs along the road tell me that I am only fifteen miles from Blu's. Since I told him I would arrive tomorrow, I turn around after four miles and head back to Liquid Louie's (*honest*) for a greasy chicken dinner washed down with a frosty rum and coke.

The scene at the local watering hole is lively with a mix of conversation and cowboy music playing on the juke box. The bartender inquires about my mode of transportation as I had parked my bicycle just beyond the window and I keep turning to keep a watchful eye on it. When I tell him that I have ridden from Steamboat Springs, Colorado and am heading north toward the border, he raises his eye brows and offers to refill my drink; on the house! I recall way too many nights from my youth that began this way and thank him for his offer as I pay for my meal and depart.

I know I will have a comfortable few nights ahead of me so I lazily set up my tent among the towering pines. The late afternoon light falls through the trees and makes patterns on the forest floor. Two hawks circle above me as I walk to the lake to view the sunset. Perched on a boulder, I watch the crimson sky turn to indigo before cautiously retracing my steps to the campsite hoping I am not being followed by some uninvited guest, like a grizzly. Later that night I hear what sounds like bears rummaging near my campsite and I clutch my bear spray tightly in one hand.

I lay in the misty dark listening to the night while thinking about today's eighty-five-mile ride. I drift off to sleep comparing yesterday's journey in which I rode sixty-five percent of it up hill today's ride where I rode sixty-five percent on flat terrain with only an occasional bumpy spot to change the pace. The next thing I know, I am waking to the light of dawn streaming in through the eastern portal of my little tent.

I dress in shorts, T-shirt and a light jacket and pedal off to have some coffee and cereal at the Swan Lake Café. I discover that they are not open for breakfast, but the proprietor at the store next door offers me a cup of coffee. She tells me there is an unmarked back road only seven miles away that will lead me into Big Fork. It is less traveled, has no trucks and, since I have plenty of time to explore, I take this unexpected option.

I find the road and follow its winding path through the trees, next to a river which turns into a lake. I pass a few very nice private homes, but see no signs anywhere. I let instinct be my guide until I look at my odometer and see that I have gone eighteen miles. I doubt myself for a few minutes before proceeding down a hill and am blown away at the vista of lakes, rivers and a small picturesque town nestled at the bottom. Immediately, I know why Blu has chosen to leave Vail and settle in this piece of paradise.

Pedaling across the single-lane wooden bridge, I wonder what the next few days will bring. I welcome the chance to visit with an old friend and perhaps make a few new ones. When I pass the marina at Bigfork Harbor, I see very little activity and few boats. In spite of the warm sunshine, I remember that summer is over and the vacation crowd has packed up and gone back home. I lean my bike against a tree and walk towards the water. A friendly stranger shares a few facts about the area as if he is from the tourist bureau. He tells me that I have just crossed Swan River and am in front of Flathead Lake. The lake is both snug and deep enough for fairly large boats to dock. He points to my left and says that the town of Bigfork is a short walk from anywhere a boat can be moored. He ends his brief introductory tour by pointing to Swan Mountain Range looming in the distance. I ask if he has a boat on the lake and he nods his head, but says today he will be taking it out of the water for the season. He waves good-bye and walks back toward the water.

Pedaling at a slow pace, I spot Blu's restaurant, Showthyme, a short distance down the main street. The restaurant is closed so I maneuver past the colorful potted plants and swaying aspen trees toward the back and get off my bike to stretch and look around. Within minutes

Blu's smiling face, beefy frame and extended hand greet me with the warmth of an old *amigo*. He proudly shows me his establishment. It is a remodeled, old two-story building with an authentic brick front and wood planks in the back that lead to a patio bordered with summer blossoms of red, pink and purple. Inside there is a small bar with a few round tables and bench seating covered in a Caribbean colored fabric of turquoise, red and yellow. A nicely detailed bistro restaurant is just beyond with a roomy, show kitchen. The storage area is in the back.

Blu tells me that Jim and Nancy Reinicke, old friends from Vail, are also living nearby. Blu writes Jim's phone number on a piece of paper, gives me directions to his house, and then tells me to make myself at home and we will meet up later. It is clear that Blu has work to do, so I pedal down the road.

Blu's place is easy to find, so once inside, I set my things down and the first thing I do is find a phone and give Jim a call. I tell him I have been riding my bike up from Colorado. He tells me that he saw a biker on the road yesterday when he and his wife were driving back home. He is most impressed that someone my age is pedaling through this rugged terrain. He insists that they are going to pick me up in an hour for lunch and a sightseeing tour of the area.

Jim was a custom-home builder in Vail. As we drive around the vicinity, we discuss the cost of property and building here in the mountains of Montana. I find out prices are equivalent to the asking prices in the Vail Valley. At this moment, I wonder if this trip is about looking for a new destination to relocate – a place to put down roots once again. I will ponder this thought later when I have long stretches of road to cover and no one but myself to converse with, but for now, I am in the company of a couple of charming friends who are introducing me to their world.

They continue to explain that the lake causes the temperatures to be warmer in winter than the towns farther away. The big snowstorms often hit around them, dumping little snow on Bigfork. In spite of this, Bigfork has not become a year-round resort. It is a summer haven for folks who revel in the outdoors. There is an abundance of fishing, boating and hiking in the mountains nearby. Business, however, dries up in the winter.

Blu later told me that he brought some people with him from Vail to open and help run his restaurant, but with almost no business eight months a year they were forced to eventually move on. He has tried to remain open during the long, lean winters, but has decided to reduce his staff this winter and open for only three to four nights a week. He and his wife supplement their income and try to keep some of the staff working by catering parties during the slow months. This tells me that, even though there is little snow in Bigfork during the winter; it is cold and unappealing to tourists.

I ask about skiing and Jim tells me that Big Mountain is only forty miles away and is the largest ski area in Montana. This, however, has few runs to compare with the ones we all enjoyed in the old days in Vail. Jim and I reminisce about working together as president and vice-president of Ski Club Vail. Back in those days, all organized skiing either was under the wing of Vail Associates or the Ski Club. While at the helm, Jim and I started a senior race program and took the Town of Vail races to new heights. The other arm of the ski club, that has remained strong to this day, is the ski coaching and race organization for kids from seven years old to young adults. We and other members of the board supported the coaches so that they could do their jobs and not spend hours caught up in the politics of the mountain. There was a lot of pressure on the coaches from the parents to produce world-class racers and the coaches needed all the support they could get. We worked with the town to get the new ski club building constructed, and of course did our share of coaching and skiing during Vail's glory days.

I reminded Jim that I was once listed as guardian for his son, Kirk, when he was going to school and racing in Aspen. Since I was living in Aspen at the time, Jim asked me to look out for him, so I was listed as next of kin in case of an emergency. This may have been as close as I got to being a parent figure.

We all make a plan to meet at Blu's restaurant for dinner on the patio, and to spend a few days with him and Nancy at their house on the hill.

The next day Jim picks me up at Blu's house and takes me to his home. Jim and Nancy constructed their dream mountain retreat overlooking enormous Flathead Lake and golf course. As they show me each room in the house, I am particularly impressed with the rock and stone detail in the interior, along with Nancy's decorating talents. I get the feeling that this is a place where fun and tranquility go hand-in-hand. Their warmth and hospitality makes me feel very welcome and like a member of the family.

When I am finished settling in, I make my way over to the outside deck where Jim and Nancy are enjoying an afternoon beverage and snack. I drop into a lounge chair, and, a few seconds later, I am recounting the experiences I have lived over the last week on my bicycle journey north from Colorado. As the light of day fades and the sky turns into a field of stars, my plans are drastically changing before my eyes.

Jim cautions me about camping in Glacier National Park, as a grizzly bear mauled a camper last week and there have been other bear sightings in the park as well. I am aware that the bears are bulking up in preparation for the upcoming winter when they will hibernate and live off of the fat they can accumulate in the fall. I don't want to eliminate Glacier from my itinerary, but I do not want to become part of the grizzly's diet either. Jim senses my disappointment and offers to take all of us for a tour of the park in his car. Nancy offers to prepare a picnic lunch with all the delicious leftovers from dinner. We will leave early in the morning. I am tired, even though I did not turn the pedals on my bike today and feel myself drifting into sleep.

It is a strange feeling not to be getting on my bike again this morning as we all pile into Jim's comfortable SUV. We talk about my plans that I formulated in the early morning hours when I awoke. I tell them that when we return to Bigfork, I will head up to Whitefish by way of Kalispell. The next day I will locate Jon and Patti Bos and possibly take the train to Seattle to visit some friends who have moved there from Vail. They add that their son Kirk also lives in Seattle. They tell me about the San Juan Islands, Victoria and the beauty of the Vancouver area. This begins to open even more possibilities for the days ahead, but for now, we have the most spectacular scenery to date just outside our window.

I am stunned with the beauty that is opening up before our eyes as we enter Glacier National Park. The mountains live up to the name Rocky, and I am thrilled to see glaciers in the distance and snowfields beside the road as we climb higher and higher on the Going-to-the-Sun Highway. We stop to have our picnic on the stony beach at McDonald Lake where perfect skipping stones line the shore. Jim and I don't miss the opportunity to have a bit of competitive play to see who has the best technique. Clearly, Jim has had more practice and his stones skim the surface of the water at distances beyond mine. After a tasty lunch, we continue. Mile after mile I am increasingly grateful that I am in a car and not on my bicycle as we climb up this narrow road with a snaking river far below.

Near the summit, we stop for a few photos in the chilly mountain air. I get the opportunity to be almost at arm's length from a mountain goat with some good size horns. I smile and know this is a far cry from the grizzlies I pictured visiting my campsite. We travel on to St. Mary's Lake at the far eastern end of the park where it borders the International Peace Park. The view of the lake and the mountains surrounding it are so beautiful that it takes my breadth away. There is a large rustic mountain lodge on the shore, but we don't take the time to explore it. I am making a silent vow to return to this park some springtime with Moe when the snow is melting and the waterfalls are pounding down the craggy mountainside.

The next day is Sunday. What a better way to spend the day than on the couch in front of the television watching football from morning till night. At half-time, I slip away to check my bike to see that the tires, seat, water bottles and panniers are ready for tomorrow's journey to Whitefish. Again I find myself ready to resume my journey and am keyed up about the days ahead.

KALISPELL, WHITEFISH
AND PLACES BEYOND

seven

I said my good-byes and walked out to my bike in a landscape that shimmered in the light and heat of the morning. I am excited to be back on my bike and find comfort in riding again today through the mountains of Montana.

Within an hour, I will be seeing several of my old friends from Vail and Aspen, circa 1980s. At eight miles an hour, I have a lot of time to think about the past: mistakes I made; things I might have done differently; actions I thought were cool, but were they really? I find myself reflecting on the negative aspects of my youth. Meeting friends from this period of my life makes me wonder how often the decisions I made influenced the friendships I kept. Sometimes I wish I could delete some of the memories that seem to remain on the hard-drive of my brain and others are so vague that it  frightens me. I am recalling stories and think that perhaps I may owe Jon and Patti an apology for something I said or did. I think back and remember how accepting they both are and begin to relax.

Jon, like me, left traces of his life in Vail before moving to Aspen. This jovial soul was a bit of a mountain man; a hunter and a spinner of tall tales. He arrived in Vail to join some of his old buddies, Paul Testwuide and the Garton brothers, from Sheboygan, Wisconsin. Not unlike the others, his good-natured, sometimes inappropriate words got him in trouble with the powers that be. As I recall, he was escorted out of town by the local authorities and soon made his way farther west to Aspen.

When I took over a few years later as general manager of a restaurant/bar complex in Aspen, Jon was working as the bar manager of one of the businesses in the complex, Alice's Alley and had made it a successful watering hole. This success was partly a result of his charismatic personality, love of life and ability to draw a local following, much like John Donovan did at the Copper Bar in Vail. I was delighted to have him as one of the key employees of the complex. It didn't take long for him and Patti to meet. She was working as a hostess next door at another establishment in the complex, the Aspen Mine Company. They left Aspen in the late '80s and moved as pioneers to this small ski area near Whitefish. A few others from Aspen and Vail followed their footsteps north.

From Big Fork, I arrive in the town of Kalispell in less than two hours and locate the 1st Ave. Bar and Restaurant, a place that Jon told me by phone that he and Patty own. This is a newly acquired establishment for them. I stop to have a look after taking a quick glance at the rapidly growing town. This little bar and restaurant has a gambling license and is referred to as a casino.

They are not open for business at this hour so I let the friendly service people know I am just peeking in and will be back at another time with the owners who are friends of mine. I am surprised at the size of the town. As I cruise through on my bike, I spot a Costco, Kmart, Wal-Mart and other large, national retail chains and a hint of some light industry, as well as the airport for all the surrounding towns. I continue on to Whitefish, my destination today.

This neat little town has an eight-mile-long and half-mile-wide lake on the outskirts. Curiosity pulls me along the quaint side streets until I spot Mark King's woodworking shop and stop in to see yet another buddy from the old days in Vail, Colorado. Mark has heard from Jon and Patti that I am traveling north and will be arriving in Whitefish before the snow falls, but he did not realize that I would be riding a bicycle and carrying all my own gear.

Mark makes his living building and designing very fine, custom wood furniture and has a long list of proud owners of his craftsmanship in the area. He stops working and we sit and reminisce right there in front of a big wooden sign on the outside of the building that says: Mark King & Friends.

I bring up the Glendesprung Competition that took place in Vail one snowy day, many moons ago. Tom Leroy and John Purcell were organizing a pro-televised ski competition and Vail Associates (operators of the ski area) wanted Ski Club Vail to test-drive the venue they had created on the mountain. I was vice-president of the Ski Club at the time and was in charge of the amateur events that were scheduled to take place in the same venue. Vail Associates was adamant that they did not want anyone to do flips on their mountain, and it was my responsibility to see that the rules were adhered to. I was stationed in the landing area along with the judges. I held the microphone and announced the skiers as each one approached the start. The skier announced to the starter what trick he would be performing; the starter relayed the information to me. When the message that Mark was doing a forward-flip reached me, I knew that there were others back in the Vail Associates offices who would be flipping out when they got the news of the afternoon's events.

Mark knew that, for the jump he was going to execute, he needed enough speed to get off of the jump and carry the flat to the fall line. In order to do this, he would have to carry a lot of speed to get the distance necessary. If he landed on the flats, he could seriously hurt himself. In the spirit of the '70s, he let it all hang out! When I announced his intention, followed by the magnificent landing on his feet, the applause assured his victory. Luckily no one was hurt, so Vail Associates kept quiet about the matter and life went on.

This story was hard to top and Mark had to get back to work so I say good-bye after we agree to meet later in the week. I pedal off down the road.

I decide to continue riding to the golf course restaurant to try to connect with Jon and Patti. I slide into the parking lot at the golf course and, within minutes, Jon pulls up next to me in his gray, GMC Suburban, with identifying plates that say *Jon Bos*. He suddenly realizes that my bike is not a Harley-Davidson and that I have pedaled my Jamison Coda bicycle all the way from Steamboat Springs, Colorado. I have noticed that when people see a fifty-year-old man riding a bike loaded with gear, it immediately breaks the ice and people warm up right away.

Jon takes me inside and proudly shows me around the casual, yet elegant restaurant. I can hear cheerful voices of the stylish clientele that are beginning to flow through the room. I spot Patti coming out of the kitchen, followed by the sound of clinking spoons. She has just finished setting up for a banquet and can spare a few minutes to sit down and join us for lunch. Lush green and flowering plants are surrounding us and a vase of summer flowers is perched in the center of our white marble table. This very attractive, proud woman tells me she used to be the mayor of Whitefish, but she is now clearly passionate about the businesses she and her husband have started and are operating together. They are legends in these parts and I am a bit green with envy over their success and fortitude in a business where I also dedicated many years of my life.

The golf course has thirty-six holes, and Patti explains that besides this one-hundred-and thirty-five-seat restaurant and bar they run several snack bars around the course. They have worked hard to develop a fine reputation in this trendy, small town. Unlike many tourist areas, Whitefish does not have many restaurants because the existing liquor licenses cost so much to buy out and new ones are only issued if the population grows considerably. I easily calculate the figures and know their business is quite successful. The move here has paid off, not only financially, but personally as well. After lunch, we make a plan to meet Patti at their house later that night. Jon puts my bike in the GMC and takes me on a personalized tour of his town and surrounding area which leads to their house.

The three-tiered house is situated on three lots overlooking the lake. They bought it many years ago as an unfinished, fixer-upper and have really done a superb job of finishing the project. From the looks of it, they have turned this property into a million-dollar home with a stunning view of Flathead Lake.

The amazing thing about this 400-foot deep lake is that the surrounding houses get all of their water directly from it. The water for drinking comes through a simple dirt-catching filter and it meets all the health standards. Jon brings his young son along and grabs his little yellow dog. The four of us head out in his boat for a ride around the lake before meeting another face from the past in town for dinner.

Ron Addlington, who worked for us in Aspen, joins us for dinner and old stories and lies are told deep into the night. Jon recalls the time he heard a noise out on the back stairwell of the bar complex and went out in the inky blackness and found me on the ground fighting for my life with a bartender from the Slope restaurant whom I had just fired. The individual refused to leave without doing battle first. Jon's appearance and extra stature saved my ass by helping to convince him that he was outnumbered and it really was time to depart the premises now!

I follow with a rendition of a story that took place on the afternoon I invited Aspen Mine Company's all-girl softball team and their competitor into Alice's Alley. They had proudly beaten their challenger from Little Annie's, another local's bar, and didn't require much encouragement to begin the celebration. I told Jon to open the beer taps and put the tequila bottles on the bar. The lax attitude of the police in those days in Aspen gave an outrageously spontaneous gathering, which would have been outlawed anywhere else, a positive nod of approval. The inspiration derived from this party took our girls' team to the championships and the parties became weekly affairs after each win.

Jon, an avid hunter and fisherman, has plans to go hunting early in the morning. I understand his not wanting to cancel his plan because

I know of his passion for this sport. I feel lucky to have the morning to relax before meeting Ron for a late breakfast. Ron also lives on the lake in a beautiful house with his wife, Barbara, an ex-waitress from Aspen, and their son. He is contemplating buying a cab company that is for sale, and since I owned and operated Louie's Casual Cabs in Vail for many years. He has asked me if I will go with him to meet the owner to discuss the deal. After the meeting, I explain all the pit-falls and fuzzy areas of the deal. We mull over the pros and cons and Ron decides that maybe the investment may not be worth the possible gains. I hope I helped steer him in the right direction.

We switch gears and head off for yet another meal at the golf course. Patti is able to join us and I learn more about what Whitefish has to offer as well as some of the negatives of living in the area.

After lunch, I pedal around town partly to work off all the rich meals I have been treated to and partly to regroup. I begin to think about the next phase of my journey. I am getting itchy and realize it is time to continue my bike adventure. It is now the middle of September; the nights are cold and I have lingered way too long in the mountains. It's time to think about beating the winter weather in the Cascades. I need to make some headway and reach the coast before riding north. I stop at the Amtrak train station and investigate the possibility of boarding a train westward with my bicycle in tow. I don't want to miss this part of the country by sleeping on a train so after three different tickets are written, I pay $178 for passage that is good to use for forty-five days. Because of my timing, I feel this is the best option and I think a quick stop in Idaho needs to be made so I can see what that area has to offer. I won't be leaving for a few days, so I have a little more time to relax and visit with new and old friends.

Ron is the head of food and beverage at Big Mountain ski area on the outskirts of Whitefish. He invites me up for a gondola ride and tour on Wednesday afternoon. I ride up to the ski mountain along a two-lane road and pass quite a few classic wooden lodges and homes before I reach the parking lot and find Ron waiting for me. I am glad that I have taken him up on his generous invitation to spend the afternoon with him.

Before I meet up with Ron, I have a relaxing lunch with Mark. During lunch, we have the unexpected surprise of running into Otis Glazeboy, someone I knew from Vail in the '60s and '70s. He said he heard that I was in town and has been trying to track me down for days now. And speaking of tracks, as soon as I see his face I am reminded of the story of how this man got tire marks on his forehead. The story that followed Otis for more than three decades took place on Bridge Street in Vail during the '70s. Otis had a heavy night of drinking and passed out on the street. He did not wake up until a Volkswagen beetle drove over his forehead and left an impression of the tires (still visible today) along with a fierce headache. Otis has not had a drink in eleven years and has just started an architecture company in town. We spend an intense hour together talking about the past and present. When he gets a phone call, he disappears in what seems to be a nano-second and I never run into him again.

Back on the mountain, I find the vistas are expansive and the sky every bit as big and blue as the day before. The clouds start rolling in while I am getting a bird's eye view of the countryside through a telescope that is set up on the deck outside the restaurant. Ron comes out and joins me on the deck. He explains that sometimes you find yourself skiing above the clouds where the sky is blue, and, below you, the town can just as easily be enshrouded with a thick cloud cover. The legend of the snow ghost becomes quite vivid as Ron explains just how wet the snow often is and how it sticks to the trees and gives the impression of ghostly creatures lurking in the shadows on this massive mountainous landscape.

Later that night, I join Patti at the home of a friend who is celebrating his birthday. This turns out to be another night of great food, good wine and very welcoming people. My Magiverish skills come in handy tonight as I suggest that we go into Noel's workshop and use one of his power drills to open that magnum of wine that has one of those corks that just won't come out. We stop to look at his trophy room that is a separate one-story building next to his garage/workshop. He, like many of the men in Montana, take hunting very seriously and proudly displays the fruits of his labor. Mountain goats, big horn sheep, turkey, elk and deer were among the pairs of eyes that seemed to light up as the space is illuminated. I have my camera along and offer to be the photographer for the evening.

I am glad that I am able to drop off copies at their house the next day of all the photos I took at the birthday party. This gesture gives me an opportunity to thank them for being so welcoming to me.

I spend my last few nights at Mark's house and we take a drive to Kalispell to have a drink at Jon's Casino and dinner at a Vietnamese restaurant around the corner. We eat and drink too much which is often the custom when visiting old friends from the past. Somehow we manage to reach his house safely. The next day, Mark offers me his car and I accept in hopes to explore a section of this magnificent country that my friends have not already introduced me to. It feels strange to be behind the wheel of a car after so long. I realize that I do not have a strong desire to switch places with any of my friends and trade my bicycle for this shiny new car. I glance up at the blue sky and reflect on the weather I have experienced so far. I decide to stop and buy some rain gear just in case my luck does not hold out when I reach the coast. I feel strongly that I am ready to get back on my bike and ride, but first, I will cross this rocky section of the country by train in order to arrive at the Pacific Northwest.

I take a few minutes to telephone the family I am going to visit once I reach the west coast. They tell me they have been expecting a call from me. Four letters from Moe have preceded my arrival. I pull out the photo I have been carrying of Moe in my wallet and know I need to put some thought into how I feel about her and how I will respond to the letters that are waiting me across the mountain passes. Visiting my happy friends from Montana and seeing how beautiful it is to share your life with someone, helps me realize that I want to be with Moe.

September 17th, the day of departure finally arrives. I bundle up my gear once again in my panniers and ride into town. I decide to take my bike to a shop to have it broken down and packed in a carton for transporting by train. I watch the procedure and know that next time I will save the $18 and do it myself. Once at the train station, I make the mistake of telling the clerk that I put a few things other than the bike inside the carton, and he makes me take some of them out: bicycle only. Live and learn!

I bid fare-well to Patti, and make another grave mistake by deciding to pass the time before the train departs by getting into a poker game at a down-town bar. An hour later, as I board the train, my wallet is $250 lighter.

RIDING THE RAILS
WESTWARD TO
THE PACIFIC OCEAN

eight

The sleek silver-and-red Amtrak train pulls in around dusk and I watch the uniformed young men roughly place my boxed-up Jamison Coda in one of the storage cars. I am one of the last to step on board the sparsely-filled train. Since I had purchased a forty-five-day Amtrak pass, I am not assigned a specific seat. With this flexible ticket I am able to get on and off an Amtrak train as I choose. This suits my style at this moment in time.

I have already scouted out the observation car with the transparent roof and move toward that car to catch a glimpse of the countryside before the day draws to an end. Everyone in the car seems to be sleeping or reading, so I choose my seat based on the best viewing spot, rather than possible companionship. I tuck my two panniers above my seat and settle down for a long night's ride.

The loud speaker comes on and startles most of us. The woman with an English accent announces that we are leaving Whitefish, Montana and will reach Everett, Washington mid-morning with a stop in the middle of the night at Sandpoint, Idaho. I focus on the view outside the window, but do not even get a real feel for the passing countryside before the sun settles in the western sky. My thoughts drift off and I chuckle to myself as I recall the last time I traveled on a train.

A few years ago, after an extended stay in California, when my footsteps were leading back to join Moe in Colorado, I unexpectedly met a man who resembled a Cigar-store Indian in the bar car on a train from Truckee, California, to Glenwood Springs, Colorado. We were sharing stories as we sipped on an alcoholic potion of some kind or another and, before long he invited me to come with him to share some peyote. I did not feel I could turn down the offer as I was already in a bit of a confused state and we were buddies. We walked out onto the platform between the two cars and I felt an unusual blast of hot, dry air. He lit up and passed a pipe to me and it took only a few tokes before I realized that I was hallucinating. What seemed like hours later, I swayed back with my new *amigo* to the bar car for a few more beverages and the telling of even taller tales.

In the middle of the night, at Salt Lake City, Utah, we tired passengers were transferred from our train by bus to the harshly lit Ogden train station where we were told to wait for the train that would take us east to Glenwood Springs, Colorado and places in-between. Paranoia had set in and I was not comfortable with my new surroundings or the people around me so I placed my bags on a row of seats and tried to sleep on top of them. I woke with a start and realized that a train was departing, so I grabbed my bags and jumped on the train. The conductor checked my ticket right away and told me I was on the westbound train. Within seconds I was flying down the corridor and down the steps. Luckily, the eastbound train was just across the platform and I tentatively climbed on board as it was departing. I have no idea what happened to my Native American buddy or for that matter where he was heading, but I did leave the train that night with one great story to tuck into my memory.

I shift in my seat and look out the window as another announcement comes over the speaker and I realize that I am hungry and would also like to have something to drink, and, yes, maybe meet another interesting traveler. I am convinced that I don't want to fall asleep like I did at the train station in Ogden and miss my stop so I will need to find something to occupy me until I reach my destination. I pull my panniers down from the baggage compartment above and chuckle as I saunter toward the dining/bar car thinking about the peyote-smoking Indian of days gone by. There is only an elderly couple at one of the tables, who look like they are not far from sleep, so I sit alone and order a grilled cheese sandwich and a cold beer. I am missing the feeling of excitement and adventure that I feel when I am on my bike pedaling from one town to the next. Maybe it is the feeling of being in control that I miss or perhaps, it is the wind in my hair and the ability to stop when and where I want. I do wish I had taken this journey a little earlier in the year when the nights were not so cold and camping would have been comfortable. At this elevation, snow is a possibility at any time during the fall and late summer season.

Every once in awhile, the three-quarter moon allows me to catch a glimpse of the pine forests that line the railroad tracks between the carved stone tunnels through the mountains. I see a reflection off of a river below the tracks, and wonder why I don't have my map handy to be able to mark my route and check the name of this ribbon-like natural wonder below me.

When the English woman comes over the loud speaker again and announces that we are approaching Sandpoint, Idaho, I am awake, but weary from the long day. I grab my panniers and feel a bit lonesome departing the train without my trusty bike, which had become my steadfast companion. I will pick it up the next day when I arrive in Everett, Washington, but for now I am in a new town with a population of 10,000 people just waiting to be explored. As I walk down Main Street at 2 a.m., I realize the bars are closing and the only people on the street are the drunks who were escorted out after last-call. Experience tells me that drunks can be pushy and down-right nasty. I had heard stories about a thick element of prejudice in this part of the country and, for all I know, a Polish-American-Jack-of-all-trades might be the next target.

I keep my cool, unlike one night many years ago when I left the Bridge Street Shuffle at 2 a.m. and was confronted by a drunken man wearing ski boots. He was carrying his skis over his shoulder and using his ski poles to balance his precarious gait. He was walking close to me and, unexpectedly, turned and knocked me in the head with his skis. I grabbed his ski poles to let him know I was not pleased. He assumed the stance of a warrior preparing to take on his opponent in a duel. I made a quick get-away and removed myself from the scene.

I duck into the Pastime Café in Sandpoint for a cup of coffee and find a lively mix of chatter coming from the late-night customers. I ask around about hotel accommodations, but no one has any suggestions so I decide to scout out something for myself.

The first well-lit place I spot is a resort hotel that caters to tourists. Oddly, the lobby doors were locked, but a *No Vacancy* sign was not posted on the window or door. When I knock, Jim, the night manager, responds and lets me in. This tall, blond youth tells me that a kids' soccer tournament is taking place this weekend in Sandpoint and the hotel has no vacancies. Jim disappears and comes back a moment later with a phone and a directory. He kindly calls around to other hotels in the area and finds a room for me for the night at a Super 8 Hotel. He even calls the only taxi available at this time of night and, after paying the $4 fare, I am on my way to what turns out to be a very restful night.

While falling asleep, I have flashbacks of the many nights when I owned Vail's first taxi company, Louie's Casual Cabs. I advertised twenty-four-hour service, and, during the summer months and off-season, there was not enough business the first year to hire another driver to make the infrequent runs so that left me in charge of making those two o'clock runs. The first thing I ask at the front desk clerk the next morning is, "Where can I rent a bike?"

The receptionist's negative response tells me that a bike rental shop might be a business I could get into. Just one more idea if I decide this is where I want to put down roots, but perhaps I have to check out the area first and meet some of the local population. I surprise myself with these thoughts as I have forgotten that part of the reason for making this journey is to investigate the country west of Colorado, including Sandpoint, Idaho, to see if I can find a place to begin the next chapter of my life; unless of course, Moe welcomes me back in her life in Colorado. This area has many of the things that interest me such as: a body of water, a mountain for skiing and hiking, clean streets and public transportation. I realize there is a lot I don't know about Sandpoint, Idaho and it is time to investigate.

I resign myself to the fact that I will not be touring the area on bike and I take a cab to the edge of the lake and stroll along the winding path that leads to the public beach and dock. This is another perfect day with a light breeze and a bright blue sky which is patched with large fluffy clouds. I wonder how many days are this pleasant here on the lake. A variety of trees, as if painted in shades of red, orange and yellow, line the fence that separates the grassy picnic areas from the sandy shoreline. I see only a few joggers and dog walkers who don't show much enthusiasm as I greet them in passing. Perhaps everyone is at the soccer fields watching the tournament? I smile and am glad the park and lake are not crowded with noisy children.

I walk the shoreline and kick up some of the fine yellow sand on the public beach. The entire area is spotless and I notice a few trash cans along the seawall. A half-dozen people from two to fifty are sitting or standing on the dock and not one of them has put his toes in Lake Pend Oreille. The lifeguard stand is vacant and I am reminded that summer is over and the water must be very cold already. The air feels like Indian summer to me and I am thrilled to be near a lake. I see that the Edgewater Hotel is open for lunch and I am tempted to head inside and find a table with a view.

Before I go inside, I spot an area where a dozen or more powerboats and an equal number of sailboats are anchored near a dock. I wander over to have a look. I have always loved being close to the water and, as a teenager living in Michigan, I spent summers at our lake cottage and was eventually the first kid in my crowd to own a water ski boat.

When I was sixteen, I earned enough money to buy a fourteen-foot boat that was designed like a Budweiser racing craft with a seventy-five horsepower Evinrude engine, the biggest outboard you could buy at the time. This sleek boat was designed for a driver, a passenger, and a water-skier. On one bright spring day, I decided to hitch her up to my car and see if any of my buddies were interested in skipping school with me and heading to the lake to water ski. I don't recall who jumped at the offer, but they all knew I had a fake ID, the boat, the car and money to buy beer to take on the road for the hour-long drive to the lake. With no other boats on the lake, the water was like glass. I drove the boat at first so that my buddies could all get a turn to ski before I decided to which one I would entrust the wheel so I could get my fill on the boards. This little boat was so powerful that it went from zero to forty miles per hour in six seconds. I remember how we skied until our legs could not hold us up any longer and, when the beer was gone and the sun was setting in the faded sky, we headed back to Detroit.

I see no one near any of the moored boats, but notice a sign pointing to a booth that sells tickets for lake cruises. A big old school bus, painted white with the red letters *Lake Cruises,* lets me speculate this might be a profitable summer business. I decide to buy a ticket to pass the day. It looks like this is as close as I will get to see Schweitzer Ski Area located across the lake. Schweitzer is closed for the off-season and will not open until November for skiing so I have obviously missed this window of opportunity. The tour departs at 2 p.m. which gives me enough time to have lunch at the Edgewater Hotel. I walk to the edge of the deck, put my bags down and lean out to gaze at the unfamiliar view. A friendly waitress at the hotel restaurant greets me and shows me to a table. There is a hum of conversation around me and I am feeling comfortable as I sit down and glance at the menu. She and the other wait staff are very engaging. After seeing my bike panniers, they ask what I am doing in these parts. They encourage me to tell them stories about my bicycle journey. They even offer to store my bags in the restaurant while I am on the boat cruise.

The boat, simply called *Sandpoint,* is three years old and seats 150 passengers. I check out the dining area and can tell that the bar has been stowed away as the regular summer *Budweiser Cruises* are no longer taking place. I can hear some clanking of dishes in the back and see two waiters casually sitting at one of the tables. I imagine they are talking about the scant crowd aboard and the lack of tips they will go home with today. I slip back upstairs to the viewing deck lined with seats only partially filled. I notice that the Captain is alone in the wheelhouse and, looking around; I don't see any other crew. I knock on the window and Dave motions for me to come in and join him.

This tall, slender, sun-tanned sailor with a gregarious personality does not seem to be in his element. He starts talking to me right away and says that he and his wife, who was making the noises in the kitchen upstairs, are longing to sell the boat and move to the Caribbean to see if they can get a sail boat charter company off the ground. They are tired of winter and they feel that it is time to see what adventures they can find on the open seas. As we share stories about our lives, he can see that I am also looking for something and, since I have already experienced island living, perhaps I may be interested in operating a business on a high mountain lake near a ski area. He lets me know that he has a continuous five-year lease on the boat and the eighteen-passenger bus and would be willing to sell his business for $300,000. I tuck the idea into the back of my mind and we continue to chat about the thirty-five-mile long, 1,600-feet deep lake. He is delighted to tell me that the US Navy has been testing submarines and sonar in the lake since 1942.

We cruise by an interesting house along the shore with a dock and a handful of boats moored out front. Dave explains that only thirty percent of the shoreline can be built on because of its rocky nature. There are two hardy souls swimming near the dock and I shiver until my new friend tells me that the lake maintains a temperature of eighty-one degrees all year long. Can this possibly be true or is this a sales tactic? The cruise takes about one and a half hours and I feel fortunate to have met and spent the time with Dave, who shared so much information about the area with me. We say goodbye and I walk back to the Edgewater Hotel. I now have a little more background about the area and think it is certainly a beautiful spot to dream about. Perhaps I will bring Moe back to Sandpoint one day and tour the area by car.

The wait staff gives me a friendly greeting when I return for my bags and I decide to have that crab leg special with a glass of chilled white wine out on the deck while watching the full moon climb over the mountains in the distance. The full moon has always been a special time for Moe and me, and I drift back to the time we were in Costa Rica at Lake Arenal hot springs watching the volcano erupt and the full moon cresting over it. I chuckle when I remember the full-moon night we spent in a *pousada* near Lisbon, Portugal. Our room was located in the upper level of the old castle and the full moon was shining in the sky just outside. I moved our bed next to the window to get a better view. Moe was a bit embarrassed at first, but how could she not appreciate the romance in my gutsy move?

I grab my bags and rush over to the train station, a ten-minute walk, and discover, not to my surprise, that the train is late. I pass the time glancing through a photo gallery of shots of the area. I have missed so many incredible sights, like the longest wooden bridge in the United States, the shopping mall built on the bridge at Sand Creek, Schweitzer Ski Area and many high mountain trails and lakes just waiting to be explored. I will note that in order to fully appreciate this area, you need to rent a car and venture off the beaten path. I fight to stay awake, and when I finally get on board, all I want is to close my eyes. Sleep is not far behind.

I awake groggy and glance out the window and find I am in the Cascade Mountains and the changing fall colors are brilliant with the morning sun shining like ribbons of light. I feel a pang of guilt about not riding my bike and am itching to get in the saddle and see those fiery colors up close. I am awe-struck with the scenery outside the window and marvel at the narrow canyons, the lazy rivers, rock formations and pine forests all aglow from the changing colors of the aspens and other deciduous trees.

As we approach Everett, the terrain changes to sheer cliffs and towering mountain peaks. The train descends into a valley shrouded in a thick fog and stops at the station. I gather my panniers and step off the train, psyched about the next leg of my journey.

IN THE SADDLE AGAIN

nine

I find my bicycle stacked outside the train station among an assortment of luggage and boxes and stake my claim. I am delighted at how easily I am able to assemble the bike. At first glance, it is a glorious day and at 10:30 a.m. I am in no hurry to leave and don't want to miss anything so I cruise downtown and head north out of Everett. I see my first drive-through coffee shop and later make a note about this idea on my ever-growing list of possible businesses for future investment. The fog rolls in and the roads become narrow, I am squeezed off the pavement. This is not a good situation to be in on a bicycle so I stop at a bike shop to find out the best route to Conway. They suggest I take a back road, which is ten miles longer but there will be less traffic. I am grateful for their help and get on my way.

The fog finally lifts at 1:30 p.m. and it turns into a nice day. I pedal through areas of vast, imposing ranchlands which shows a hint of fall in the air. The copper-colored fields remind me that winter is just around the corner. I reach Conway, a two-horse town, five miles south of Mt. Vernon.

I am on my way to visit Kirk Reinicke, his wife, Kathryn, and their two school-age children. I pedal hesitantly up to their house, not knowing what I might find. I am not always comfortable with children. I have not met Kathryn and I have not seen Kirk since he was a student at the high school in Aspen at least fifteen years ago.

I again recall the time his dad called me and asked if they could put my name and phone number on his school forms as his guardian and person to call in case of an emergency. My first contact with Kirk was back in the early '70s when I was vice-president of Ski Club Vail and Kirk was an aspiring young racer. When I moved to Aspen I was not the most responsible person at the time and here was someone entrusting his most valuable treasure to me. I wonder if Kirk will remember much about me. Kathryn welcomes me with open arms and I feel right at home as she gives me a tour of the house, introduces me to the kids and we all settle down to wait for Kirk to return from work.

She silently hands me four letters from Moe. I excuse myself and go into the guest room where I will be spending the night to read the news from Colorado. Moe is obviously missing me, but she has found a way to carry on with her busy life that centers on her teenage daughter while she searches for joy in the daily routine. I feel a sting in my gut and become aware of the gaping void in my life. I will have to put a great deal of thought into what I really want for the future, but for now, I know I wish she were here by my side.

Dinner is casual. Kirk tells his wife and children a story about a ski race in Steamboat Springs where I was called in to chaperon the group of Ski Club Vail racers. Their coach had been in a car accident that required hospitalization so someone called and begged me to come to Steamboat as quickly as possible to supervise the kids. The kids were notified of their coach's condition and told that a replacement would arrive shortly to take over. The racers sighed, not knowing who would show up and how the weekend of racing would play out with their coach and mentor now in the hospital.

Kirk gives his family a little of the story background. He recounts. "At that moment, Lou received a phone call from my father, who was the Club president, asking him to step in and take responsibility for the kids. That afternoon, Lou got his shift at the bar covered and drove to Steamboat, wondering if he was the right person to be placed in charge of a group of teenagers."

Kirk continues to tell us how he and the other members of the downhill racing team had already made plans to party that night in hopes of not being supervised by an adult. With me being a seasoned professional in getting around supervision, the guys had no choice but to settle in for a night of much needed rest. I tell Kirk and his family how the guys made me feel comfortable right away and the next morning, I surprise myself by slipping easily into the role of coach. Neither of us remembers how we fared in the downhill that day, but I was feeling like a responsible adult for once in my life.

Following dinner, we watch Monday Night Football before falling into bed. I admit to them that I do miss the comforts of home and, although I am not a die-hard football fan, I enjoy watching a good game.

The morning is shrouded in a blanket of fog, and I delight in the ability to sleep in a cozy bed and not have to hang my bedding out to dry before I take off to explore for the day. Kathryn tells me not to expect the clouds to lift until late morning or early afternoon. I settle down with a cup of freshly brewed coffee and browse through a book sitting on the coffee table about the San Juan Islands and the Washington coast. I am anxious to be close to the water again and keep this in mind as I spread my maps out on the kitchen table and begin to plan my itinerary for the day.

I find just what I am looking for, a twenty-mile route through the back roads to Anacortes. I decide it is time to call an old Vail friend, Jackie Flater Wood, who is living with her family on Bainbridge Island. She sounds excited to hear from me and gives me directions to her house from Vancouver. She asks me to call when I am closer in a week or so. I smile as I see my plans for the next part of my journey shaping up. I pack the few things I have removed from my panniers and saddle up for the day's ride under a foggy cloud cover that does not seem to be receding.

I pass more of the drive-in, pre-Starbuck espresso shops and count at least twenty kiosks on the way out of Everett. I wonder how long it will take before someone opens one in Colorado ski country. I pass a Mc Donald's and notice they have created a modern sign which replaces the traditional tall, golden arches which have become an icon for my generation.

The back road I have chosen takes me on a scenic journey past old farmhouses that are being restored in rural Victorian splendor. The large number of black and white cows leads me to assume that dairy farming could be big business here and perhaps I will find a fantastic ice cream shop at the end of the road. Around a bend, I am treated to the site of snow-covered Mt. Baker towering over the valley.

Before long, I am passing through a small fishing town, La Conner.

It has become a bit of a tourist trap with an amazing amount of charm. As I meander through the main street, I see that more of those old Victorians are being renovated and antiquated buildings are being turned into restaurants and shops. I spot a large marina as I approach the coast and notice signs leading to the Indian reservation on the other side of the river. These two neighboring communities must create a very diverse and interesting population.

I quickly reach my destination of Anacortes, a sprawling community with renovated buildings interspaced with new ones. An antique, three-story hotel is the focal point of town along with many homes on the side streets which are also being restored. The big sign that indicates that you have arrived in Anacortes is surrounded by green grass and colorful blossoms with no hint of the season's change approaching. I pedal along until I reach the ferry docks.

I stand awestruck, looking at the massive dock and locks built for the Washington State Ferry System. I find out when I take one of the free brochures that I am about to embark on a boat that is part of the largest ferry system in the United States and the third largest in the world. Twenty–four million people ride the twenty-eight vessels a year, as compared to the 20,000,000 that ride the Staten Island Ferry. I realize I am standing at only one of the twenty ferry terminals from Port Defiance (Tacoma) in the south to Sydney in the north. The ferries transport freight as well as many others like me who use them as a means of touring.

I also pick up a map of the San Juan Islands and a ferry schedule at the Anacortes docks. I see that the next ferry for the Islands will depart at 3:30 and it is now 3 p.m. I note that the Island I have chosen to visit first, Orcas, is shaped somewhat like an Orca whale or, more realistically, a horseshoe. I have chosen Orca for my first stop because it is one of the largest Islands in the chain and should provide a good biking experience, has a campground and Jim Reinicke tells me not to miss seeing the beautiful Rosario Resort.

The San Juan Islands, located in the lower reaches of the Puget Sound, include a cluster of four fairly large to medium islands and over 100 smaller ones which do not have names on my map. A guy who lives on Orcas has struck up a conversation with me and tells me that I should find most of my days on the Island sunny; in fact, the Island has less than half the rain you would experience in the neighboring city of

Seattle. He is an artist in one of the colorful hamlets overshadowed by the towering peaks of Mt. Constitution. I imagine that he is a landscape painter by the way he describes the lush forests, farms, valleys, placid lakes and stunning mountain views which wrap around a gorgeous fjord.

I hold my $7.30 ticket as I board the 800-passenger ferry (ten per cent occupancy today) with my bicycle at my side. The ferry finally departs at 5 p.m. and stops at Lopez Island to drop off and pick up passengers before we reach Orcas an hour and a half later. I recall that an old Vailite, Mitch Hoyt, for whom I used to work lives on this Island. I will ask around to try to locate him later in the trip.

Next stop is Shaw Island. I am getting very excited as I see all the activity around the port. The more I see, the more I realize how much people pass up in their lives. They get stuck in the everyday tasks of working and living. I am happy that I have chosen this route of discovery and I did not even have to leave the country.

When the ferry finally arrives at Orcas, I know it is only a twenty-minute bike ride to my *hotel under the stars*, but I feel anxious and a bit concerned as I glance at the clock on the station wall and realize that darkness will soon settle in.

ISLAND FEVER

ten

Winston Churchill once said that the San Juan Islands are a perfect destination for people like himself, whose tastes are very simple, yet at the same time, want the best of everything. Sounds like my kind of place!

I exit the ferry at Orcas Island on September 20th. Walk-ons and bicycles are escorted out first and I take note of the sun setting behind the island. I follow directions that a fellow traveler shared with me as I hop on my bike and head east for two and a half miles to a lake and camp site that he described. I see no signs for either, and the lake turns out to be more like a pond. I find a road leading in through the trees and reluctantly follow what the sign describes as a cross-country ski trail. This strikes me as very strange, as I understood that snow rarely happens here. I check out a couple of possibilities before making a choice. The pine trees in the area are so thick that I can barely see the sky or lake. Darkness has set in and I am surprisingly tired from my meager thirty-five-mile ride today. I am keenly aware that there will be no place to go for dinner, but am comforted by the fact I have a protein bar, plenty of water and the temperature is about seventy degrees as I crawl into my tent for an early night's sleep. Minutes later, I decide to take the rain cover off the tent so that I can watch the moon rise through the trees from the south and slowly cross over me and set to the north. It has illuminated the campsite and transformed it from an eerie dismal place to one with a spark of magic.

The warm sun coaxes me out of bed and onto the road early so that I can explore the beach road I saw the night before. It is a quiet and welcoming place until I reach a sign indicating I have arrived at a dead-end with only private access to the water. I sigh in disbelief, because I know the steep road back up is not going to be easy. For the first time on my bicycle journey, I am forced to dismount and walk the bike up hill part of the way.

I head north as the road turns to gravel for a couple of miles uphill, then, thank goodness, back to pavement as I approach a divide at the summit. On the other side, I am propelled down almost like being on a carnival roller coaster ride. I realize that I am smiling as I reflect on the time that I took Moe's daughter, Ailish, and her friend Ryan to Busch Gardens in Tampa, Florida to ride the roller coaster. I had recently had surgery for varicose veins and my leg was seriously bandaged. The teenage girls, were at first reluctant about pushing me around the park in a wheel chair and even having to be saddled with me, until the roller coaster attendants, after seeing me in the wheel chair, allowed all three of us to go to the front of the line each time we rode the monster!

The scene below is a delight to behold as I stop to take photographs of the small farms, a llama ranch and tiny mountain homes nestled in the tall pines. It is easy to forget that I am on an island, for no water is in view. The countryside seems to be saturated with semi-tame deer that come close to investigate a newcomer to their neighborhood. Everything looks different from the saddle of your bike and I am grateful for this opportunity to see life from a different perspective.

On my way toward Rosario Resort, a not-to-miss spot my friend recommended, I pedal through the four-block fishing village of Eastbound. There are a few quaint shops and restaurants and friendly-looking people.

I eventually see my turnoff that leads down a steep road for one and a half miles. I know the ride up is going to be as challenging as the last side trip, but I take the turn. When Jim came to Rosario, he arrived by boat where the approach from the water must be spectacular, not to mention effortless. As I approach this historical landmark, I know that I won't even bother to ask how much the rooms are.

My mind drifts back to a resort with similar architecture where Moe and I once stayed on one of my backdoor tours of the Samana Peninsula in the Dominican Republic. After having dinner and dancing to Bob Marley at a *palapa* restaurant on a beach at the end of the peninsula, we wound our way back along the road and decided to check into a stunning, new five-star hotel. The name has escaped my memory, but not the wonderful ambiance of the resort perched on the rocky shore.

Even though I know I may not have the funds to pay for a room here at the elegant Rosario Resort, I don't want to miss taking a tour of the hotel and manicured grounds. I am not disappointed, and don't mind the fact that I know I will have to struggle back up to the main road in order to reach the entrance of Moran State Park. I stop to read a description of this 5,000-acre camping park that has five fresh water lakes and over thirty hiking trails. I see that the highest point on the Island, Mt. Constitution, is located in the park and offers panoramic views of the Puget Sound and its numerous miniature islands.

I am not surprised to discover that all of the north entrance facilities and camp-grounds in the park are closed. It is only 11 a.m. and I'm not far from the southern tip of the island. The south campground is open, but it is way too early to check-in. I have only gone twenty-five miles today, and I am only fourteen miles from the ferry dock where I arrived. The up and down winding roads easily account for the discrepancy in mileage. I will return to the park in a day or two to explore its trails and natural sites. I decide to look for a restaurant in the little town of Olga, situated along the rocky shore, as my stomach is reminding me that I have not eaten since yesterday. After a tasty lunch at a beautiful old seaside restaurant, I am fortified and have renewed energy for my journey to Doe Bay, located at the opposite end of the Island from the ferry dock.

This place is a charming shadow of its former self: a 1920s village whose sole industry was the post office, with its old-style façade and fine fir floors. The building (now serving as the resort's big kitchen) faces a gentle grassy slope dotted with cabins connected by plywood and tarpaper walkways. They are not particularly aesthetic, but the ramp treatment is great for keeping the mud off your shoes. This funky hostel and sixty-acre campground, located on a rocky cliff overlooking Doe Bay, pulls me in and the $13 price for campsites is within my budget. A few skinny sea kayaks are lined up on the rocky beach and a vegetarian restaurant offers an interesting and inexpensive menu created with organic foods mostly grow on the Island and in the surrounding waters.

I scout out the landscape that includes an assortment of rustic huts and tent cabins and find a unique site to set up my tent near a rocky promontory with a stunning view of the bay and a lone sailboat moored just off shore. I notice by the sound of laughter that some of the hippy clientele are already relaxing in the 104-degree hot tubs fed by a natural mineral spring 330 feet below ground. I take some time to catch up on writing, until I am hustled by my neighbor, William, to join a volleyball game. After the game, a group of us have a little dinner in the vegetarian restaurant. I tell William about Rosario Resort and convince him to drive there for an after-dinner drink on me.

Rosario Resort is a bit stuffy for us, and the average age of the clientele is sixty-five years old, but we admire the architecture, the rich paneling and the elegant furnishings as we sip our drinks in the classic-looking bar before heading back to Doe Bay to soak in the clothing-optional hot tubs. The twenty-person, wood-fired sauna is packed, but there is always room for one more in the two open-air hot tubs and the one unheated tub. The conversation bounces back and forth from travel stories to the aches, pains and injuries of the soakers and who is going to massage whom. We all agree that this island is one of the tougher bike rides on the continent, because all of the villages, special beaches and ferry docks are on the coast and you have to pedal uphill to the main road in order to continue to the next place. Those traveling by boat have the real advantage of experiencing the beauty of the island without the physical exertion. My thoughts begin drifting far away so I quietly depart for the showers and my campsite overlooking the rocky beach and emerald green water.

I awake under a cloud of fog and am tempted to stay in my sack for a bit longer, but both my mind and body are telling me to break camp and move along to see what else the island has to offer. In the restaurant, I meet the volleyball team and we tout our win from the previous night. I take a cup of sizzling coffee and join a couple who are writers for travel magazines and books that attract cyclists from around the country. They take turns, one driving the support van while the other one rides along with the guests for their short bike trips in the area. I have a vision of Moe and myself in their jobs since Moe has a talent for writing and I, the passion for bike riding, and think this could be a possibility!

My tracks take me back to Moran State Park to explore the scenery a bit more deeply. Deer are everywhere along the road and today they pay little attention to me, the lone biker in their territory. The waters of Puget Sound are like glass and I am wishing I were out there on a water ski cutting back and forth through the wake of the boat. A couple of times Moe and I camped on an island on Lake George, New York. Our friends had a ski boat and wave runner. Robby was an accomplished skier on what was known as "the air chair." This amazing water ski is a single ski with a chair the skier sits on. The bottom of the ski has an eighteen-inch shaft connected to a small pontoon as the skier picks up speed the ski comes out of the water and the skier is using the pontoon to navigate across the wake. What an amazing sight it is to see the skier sitting and balancing himself above the water.

Three Budweiser trucks rumble by, indicating that there is still plenty of partying to be done on Orcas Island. I settle in on my Jamison Coda and check out the neighborhood. I notice that property values are not as high as I thought they might be. You can still buy a nice home with a bit of land for $300,000 to $600,000, or a lot on the water for $100,000 to $150,000. I see signs everywhere indicating that Orcas Island attracts people with a '60s mentality who are into organic gardening as well as alternative healing techniques. As I pedal around the interior of the Island, I feel like I am riding through the fir trees of Lake Tahoe. Once again, it occurs to me that I have lost sight of the fact that I am touring an island. The water in the distance looks like lakes situated between tracts of land rather than separate islands in a large body of water.

There is evidence that the timber industry is an active business on Orcas Island, as is the eighteen-hole golf course that is open year round except on an occasional snowy day. Fees for a round of golf with a cart are only $40. I love a great bargain, but since I am no longer a golfer, I will pass.

The guidebook I read this morning in the restaurant agreed with the Doe Bay crowd and said that Orcas is the hardest bike ride because of its narrow and steep roads. I am beginning to think that I will head to the ferry and move on to San Juan Island. When I discover that the price of a B&B room near the ferry is $100- $120 and lunch is $15, I know that my decision to depart for greener shores is a good idea.

I purchase my ticket for the 1:30 p.m. ferry. I am told that it will most likely be delayed because the 11 a.m. ferry has not even arrived and it finally pulls into the harbor at 1 p.m. No problem. I hop on that one instead and get a head start. Before long, I meet a biking couple, Mike and Becky from San Francisco, who also stayed at Doe Bay the night before. They did not arrive until after dark and we did not notice one another among the shadows in the soaking tubs. From stories shared by my new friends, I can tell that Becky is not as enamored with biking as Mike is. In fact, Mike makes a comment that biking at four miles an hour is not what he had in mind when he planned their bike vacation. By the time we dock at Friday Harbor on San Juan Island, we have bonded and decide to have a drink, followed by lunch together.

Before finding a restaurant, we stop at the Moped rental shop and tourist information office to find out other transportation options on this island. Their decision about where to spend the night is based on the fact that they are leaving on the 9 a.m. ferry to Victoria and need to be able to get to the ferry on time. They choose to rent a Moped and camp along the coast. I am going to follow through with my plan to go to the lake-campground where swimming and showers are available.

After a leisurely lunch on the patio of a Mexican restaurant in downtown Friday Harbor, where we share a few more rounds of travel stories, they invite me to visit them in San Francisco on my way south. We depart in separate directions. I take a wrong turn, but remind myself how much I like discovering my own secret out-of-the-way route and, before long, I have made the four-mile trip through the center of the island a ten-miler. I am delighted to discover that riding is much easier and more casual on San Juan and the temperature for mid-September is a surprisingly warm seventy-five degrees. Unexpectedly, I spot a blackberry patch next to the road and just stretch from my saddle to gather as many as I want. I imagine I will find more of these tasty treats as I meander down the road to the campground.

I pedal into Lakedale Campground and am delightfully surprised that it is composed of eighty-two acres, about half of which is water. The facilities are clean and the added luxury of a hot shower for only $1 is a treat. The season has definitely wound down and there is only about twenty percent occupancy at this $5-a-night hotel with a magnificent view of the stars and a distinctive sea smell.

I soon find that this very lively campground hums with a buzz of conversation until 10 p.m. sharp, then silence. The moon is almost full and growing bigger and brighter each night. My tent is soon glazed by moonlight and I fall asleep with the rolling motion I felt on today's ride along with the exhilarated feeling that I had reached a new, high speed of almost forty miles per hour while barreling down to the coast on Orcas Island.

I wake, once again, in dew-soaked environment and ride in search of the sun to Roche Harbor. The hotel resort and marina here have lots of history -built on 150 acres that is today a living museum. The original Hotel de Haro once housed presidents and tycoons visiting the McMillan family, founders of Roche Harbor Lime & Cement Company, Washington's oldest viable corporation. The grand, main residence now houses the restaurant and lounge where the finest in northwest cuisine is served. Considering that I am here at mid-morning and my cash is dwindling, after taking a leisurely tour of the grounds and buildings, I opt to press on and find a campground farther up the road. Every place I stop has an incredible view of the Puget Sound with at least one sailboat, piloted by a captain in an *island state of mind*, floating in the wind or moored close to the rocky shore. I ponder what this mode of transportation might be like for a return trip to the area. Because of the warm weather and absence of colorful deciduous trees in the throes of loosing their red, yellow and orange leaves, I am finding it easy to loose track of the fact that it is fall.

The San Juan Islands are in what is called a rain shadow with the

Olympic Mountains to the southwest and Vancouver Island to the west. Incoming Pacific storms drop their rain over Vancouver Island when uplifted by the mountains. The rainfall level can be only twenty-five inches a year here, while at the same time, it is dumping forty-five inches in nearby Seattle. I don't see any desalination plants on the Island and have been wondering if water for personal use comes from wells or is collected in cisterns from rain. Travel at this slow-bicycle pace gives one the opportunity to think about things like this.

I glance at the incline in front of me and settle in for another tough ride up to the main road where I see the prairie lands which encompass the American and British Camps. It is at this historic site that I learn the bizarre story of how the United States and Great Britain nearly went to war in 1859 over a dead pig. All I can think of is the great pig sandwiches Moe and I shared in Puerto Rico and for a fleeting moment I am contemplating the possibility of opening up a pig stand to cater to the tourists who come here to see a bit of history.

I can see that it is time to concentrate so I tackle the downhill with white knuckles gripping my brakes for over half mile to Snug Harbor. The reminder of the ride out is lurking in the back of my head as I pedal toward Small Pox Bay where I find a $4.50 campground at Sunset Point. This turns out to be one of the prime spots to whale watch. I am told that Snug Harbor is the best place to catch a boat to observe the whales, sea lions, seals, porpoises and bald eagles as they travel south this time of the year. I see a few serious naturalists, securely seated on the bluff over the water with binoculars in hand, hoping for a sighting. With a tone of disappointment, they tell me there have been no sightings here for the past few days.

I leave my belongings at my campsite and decide to hitch into Friday Harbor and check the ferry schedule. As I figure it, if I take the ferry to Vancouver from here I won't have to pedal that agonizing route back uphill to the center of the island. This charming walking village is loaded with art galleries, boutiques and waterfront restaurants. I treat myself to a salmon dinner and a Cadillac Margarita. After dinner, I am sure that I'm not interested in cruising the local shops so l take a shuttle van back to the north side of the Island. I don't want to leave the Island without having the opportunity to see what is on the other side.

Timing is going to be important in the morning as the only ferry to Vancouver from Friday Harbor leaves at 9:50 a.m. and the shuttle van doesn't show up at the campground until about 9 a.m. I will see what other suggestions my neighbors at the campsite have to offer.

I knew there was a reason that I don't usually plan my route too far in advance. This time fate brings me together with my campsite neighbors, a couple from Canada, who introduce me to a new and better plan than the one I was tossing around in my head as I bumped over the island roads in the van just an hour before. We exchange maps, sights to see and places to stay along the opposite routes we are embarking on in the morning.

Just as I suspect, the soppy feeling of dampness creeps over my tent, and I get up at 2 a.m. to put the fly up as the moisture has already started seeping inside. After a minute or two in the dark, my eyes adjust to the faint lantern glow streaming out of my neighbor's tent. I guess the moisture has interrupted their sleep as well. Since the shuttle van does not work out as far as time goes, I have no choice but to wake up early and pedal the ten miles to the harbor where the ferryboat will embark. Perhaps knowing I have a time schedule to keep today, I find it hard to fall back to sleep and I wake up to take off early for the harbor. Once there, I have plenty of time to do laundry, take a shower at the pay dockside facilities, dry my clothes and eat breakfast.

I am feeling some excitement about crossing the border into Canada and hopefully getting another stamp on my passport.

eleven

The ferry smoothly crosses the vast green waters of Puget Sound toward Sydney Harbor, which is only seventeen miles north of the city of Victoria on Vancouver Island. I depart from the ship with my bike and meet the Canadian custom's agent who greets me warmly and asks if I am carrying any weapons. I absent-mindedly do not mention the little container of mace I am carrying for protection from bears and other unwelcome intruders into my campsites. He smiles and says, "Have a good trip". I am convinced this is a good starting point for entering a new country, just waiting to be explored.

I am in no hurry as I ride around Sydney and notice that the town appears to be working hard to get tourists to linger instead of going straight to the Island's capital city. I stop at a bank and cash in some money and am delighted to see that the exchange rate will stretch my dollars. I also pick up ten lottery tickets and some film and quickly gobble down one of the worst hamburgers I ever ingested.

So much for hanging-out any longer in Sydney Harbor - I decide to take off for Victoria and am told by a friendly sales person in the photo shop that the coast road I am intending to ride is too narrow and suggests that I take Highway #17. I follow his suggestion for about eight miles. This road turns out not to be very scenic and quite noisy so when I see Cordova Bay Road, I take my chances. Now this is more my style and the stunning views along the coast get my heart speeding. The eye-popping vistas are starting to remind me of Highway #1 along the California coast where the Pacific Ocean views fills one with joy. I am focused on today so I will let that thought fade into the background.

It is already 2:30 p.m. so I start to look for a campground. Luckily, one is located off the road at Thetis Lake and is only $10 Canadian. I am feeling good about this lazy, low mileage day. I set up camp and look for the $1 shower. When I return to my campsite, I realize that I have neighbors! Neil and his girlfriend are Canadian and they tell me they are on a vacation, heading south with their truck and trailer. We discuss my bike trip and what I have seen over the past few weeks and they share some information they have discovered about this area. Before long, they offer me a ride into Victoria to see the sights. I am grateful to explore the city on foot without having to worry about my bike.

In Victoria we go our separate ways and I walk for miles photographing the architecture, harbor, Pedi-cabs, horse–drawn carriages, double-decker buses and boats. It is obvious that there are many different transportation choices for seeing the city, including moped rentals for $25 a day. Flowers are blooming in pots and beds everywhere and the finely-dressed appearance of the city is reflective of the recently held Commonwealth Games that are only second to the Olympics in size. I stop to rest on a bench and read a little about the history of the city and what things a tourist should not miss.

Victoria is Western Canada's oldest city and was originally settled in 1843 as Fort Victoria, a regional outpost of the Hudson Bay Company. Its harbor was home to one of the world's largest whaling and sealing fleets and a major port of entry to British North America. In the 1860s, the city blossomed like many boom towns south of the Canadian border.

The thing that impresses me at this moment is the fact that the city leaders had the foresight to protect and preserve its architecture and its fabulous gardens and parks. For instance, there are height restrictions on the buildings which make you feel comfortable rather than dwarfed. I notice that, in this people-friendly place, you can get to most locations in minutes, even on foot. Some describe Victoria as a capital city with small town charm.

I am ready to continue with my back door tour of the city. I walk over and stand in front of the Empress Hotel which seems to showcase the harbor and city of Victoria. It is built in an opulent style that was common at the turn of the 19th century and drenched with the elegance and grandeur of a bygone era. I glance at my attire and think, "What the heck!" I confidently enter the main doors and stroll around the lobby with its plush and gleaming furniture. It is not that I feel out of place, but I am drawn to the outdoors and find the exit into the lush flowering gardens. I think about putting this on my list of places to return to with Moe someday, but recall how we both prefer staying at smaller, more intimate Bed and Breakfast hotels. Maybe we could just stop in this elegant setting for a glass of wine.

I realize that there are so many intriguing spots to check out as I walk for miles within the harbor area. I am going to run out of film before I get back to the campsite if I don't show some restraint. I wonder if I am taking all these photos for my own memories, or to impress Moe that I am still able to find another fantastic travel destination. I pass a few crowded tea rooms and remember that Victoria was home to famous tea merchants around 1894. Remnants of the classic custom of afternoon tea are still alive and well in this city.

I also notice numerous English pubs scattered along Douglas Street and other side streets in the area. I stop into the Strathcona Hotel to have a drink as it offers many different choices, including the popular multi-level Sticky Wicket with a cricket theme. The bars and restaurants are laid out on three floors with eight different bars which include a pool hall, nightclub, roof top bar, English pub, sports bar and an authentic hillbilly establishment. I cruise through most of them and have only one glass of rich, dark stout poured from one of the shiny pulls lined up at each of the bars.

Walking outside, the dark blue haze of dusk surrounds me, but the streets leading back to the harbor are well lit. My thoughts are taken back a few years ago when Moe and I were traveling in Spain and spent a long night exploring the brilliantly lit fountains and buildings in the *Plaza Mayor* in Madrid before we ended our trip and flew back home. As I reach the harbor, the reflection in the dark waters of the bay of the Government House, Empress Hotel and other classic buildings offer a spectacular sight.

I am able to hop on a bus that will take me less than a mile from the campground for only $2. Before long, I crawl into my tent for a warm night's sleep and am comforted by the sound of an owl in the distance. I can't seem to wrap my mind around all I have seen in the city today, but know that I need to spend at least one more day sight-seeing in Victoria before I head for Vancouver.

I wake on Sunday to another perfectly clear, blue sky. I remove the panniers from my bike and ride into the small town a mile away to have some breakfast. I stop at a store on the way back and buy three rolls of film for almost half the price sold in the city. The scenic route back to the campground clears my head and, even though this trip is meant to give me the opportunity to reconfigure my past and make a plan for the future, it has become clear to me that all I want today is to think about this moment and all that my senses are able to absorb.

Back at the campsite about 100 yards from the lake, I relax in the sun with my eyes wrapped up in dark glasses until the noisy children and dogs force me to make a plan for the afternoon. I decide to ride my bike into Victoria via Highway #1A, which takes me the back way along a river which winds through a park before reaching Chinatown. I happen upon a crowd of Asians, including a few dignitaries, who are lined up along the street under the historic *Gate of the Harmonious Interest*. The crowd is watching a group of people assembling banners and putting on Chinese dragon costumes. I am told that this ceremony is being prepared to bless one of the buildings in Chinatown. I listen to the music and watch until I am lost in the Chinese ceremonial language and decide it is time to see what is around the corner. I never cease to be amazed at the patterns life has created around me.

I have noticed quite a large Asian population in Victoria and find out that this was the largest Chinatown in Western Canada at one time. In fact, this area once known as the *Forbidden City,* covered six city blocks and included about one-hundred-fifty businesses, three schools, a hospital, two churches, five temples, two theatres and over ten opium factories. Opium was legal in Canada until 1910. Today, Chinatown is considerably smaller, but still has a mystical feeling about it and retains the exotic charm of the Far East with its vegetable markets, gift shops and restaurants. The arch we were standing under was dedicated in 1981 to symbolize the spirit of co-operation between the Eastern and Western cultures.

I am ecstatic about all the unexpected surprises I have encountered so far today, when I happen upon one more. I am forced to dismount and walk my bike through a colorful street fair, and notice that the sound of the rushing cars is muted by the laughing voices and music from the assortment of musicians. The pavement is crowded with young couples joined at the hip, families, tour groups homogenized by race and a band of teens with I-pods. It occurs to me that I am starving so I join a line at one of the tiny food booths and order a tasty pesto pasta salad for $1.50 which turns out to be an unbeatable taste treat.

Pedaling toward the waterfront, I notice a castle-type building in the distance. This is the historic residential district I read about yesterday that includes Craigdarroch Castle. I am fascinated with the Tudor and Gothic Revival architecture of these old gems and snap lots of shots of the homes and gardens. The impressive Government House building is closed today, but the splendid old gardens are open to the public so I wrap up my tour of the city with a stroll through the multi-hued gardens.

As I fall asleep in my cozy tent, I am filled with a mixture of anxiety and excitement thinking that tomorrow I will be heading north and am not sure what I will encounter along the way.

In the morning, I crawl out of my tent and cross the campsite to get a better look at the lake under a shower of sunlight. I have developed a routine of sorts in dismantling my campsite and packing my panniers, and I go about my work without much deliberation. It is Monday, September 26th and at 7:30 a.m., it is fifty degrees and the sky is a deep blue. I take the back roads out on the west side of the peninsula along Prospect Lake Road. My bike and I wind through some small

mountains. I pass a sign beside the lake that warns me to carry chains past this point so I know that I am in for some ups and downs, but thankfully there is no snow in the forecast. Again, I feel like I am on a peaceful, moving roller coaster with very little traffic to intimidate me as I admire the old fir trees that are leading me to the entrance of the popular Butchart Gardens.

I have always enjoyed the beauty and tranquility of a colorfully laid out garden, but had no idea of the treat to which my senses were about to be presented. I pay the $11 entrance fee and move peacefully from the rose garden, to the Japanese garden, to the green houses, then on to the wild-flower beds and, last-but-not-least, find I am particularly enraptured with the idea of the sunken garden. I can imagine how this pit once held the lime deposits that were needed to make cement for the Portland Cement Plant whose home was on this site in the early 1900s.

Each garden is interspersed with statues, fountains, streams and bridges, often tucked away from the common pathways to an area beyond what the eye is able to see at first glance. I don't notice a single person on his/her knees, weeding or pruning, and wonder how the grounds could be tended before and after visiting hours. Another fascinating thing to contemplate is the fact that the gardens are open year round with special events, such as fireworks held on 4th of July and a light show presented every Christmas season.

Before I know it, I have taken over thirty photos and spent $20 on cards and seeds at the gift shop. This is something I never indulge in, but then, how much space can a few packets of flower seeds take up in my bike bags? As the friendly young girl rings up my order, I am wondering if she is one of the family members who, I am told, is still administrating this family treasure. In the 1920s, when the lime ran out, the owner's wife began planting trees, shrubs and flowers to try to bring the property back to life and here it is today, in all its glory, welcoming visitors from all over the world.

As I depart the gardens and saddle up on of my Jamison Coda, I am wondering how Moe would feel about the possibility of adding rock gardens, streams and fountains in her little mountain back yard when I come to a screeching halt. Luckily, I am pedaling uphill and do not suffer any damage to myself, but know I have to find a bike shop quickly. The back pannier rack stuck in the spokes when the screws that hold the rack onto the bike frame snapped off. I manage to rig it all together and slowly maneuver the additional three miles to Sidney where Willy, at the Harbour Prop shop, is able to help me. He repairs both boats and bikes, which strikes me as an unlikely mix. When I meet Willy, he shows me the bike frames, hanging overhead, which he builds under the name of Fahnini. Willy senses that I am feeling like a nervous parent waiting for his *baby* to be treated by a doctor. He suggests I go next door to have a bite to eat while he finishes up the *surgery*. Willy does a great job of brazing a new piece onto the frame and, to my surprise, even paints it to match the bike frame. He also reinforces the other side in case it has also started to weaken.

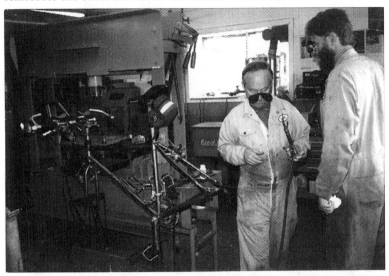

One and a half hours and $25 later, I am back on the road in time to catch the 4:30 p.m. ferry to Fulford Bay where I relax on the short ferry ride to Salt Springs Island. A fellow passenger tells me that there is a campground only a couple of miles outside of the harbor. Once on land, I am presented with two choices: the southeast campground which is located about six miles away; and the north camp, about eight miles away. I am told there is a big hill to pull going north and I am thinking that maybe it is too late to start in this direction.

I begin to wonder if I look really old today, as two different persons mentioned that I should wait until the morning to go north. I think it over in my egotistic mind and head north! I maneuver the hilly countryside scattered with farms featuring cattle and sheep grazing on small parcels of land. I make it to the north campground by 6 p.m. and set up my tent. It doesn't take long before I am able to examine my surroundings and notice that the town of Ganges seems to have spread out to the campground. I have a pretty clear view of the high school through the trees only 300 yards from my camp. A neighbor camper tells me that band practice is from 8 until 9 p.m. and the trick is to ignore it! This warning is enough to motivate me to ride into town to look for Monday Night Football, but I quickly discover that all of the sports bars are showing hockey. This certainly makes sense as we are now in Canada.

This little town which appeared to me to be nothing more than a glow on the dark earth is, in reality, quite a lively place. I notice that all of the homes and commercial property look like. They were built in the last five to ten years and there is a large population of young teens, on foot and in cars, making plenty of noise. This section of town connects to another one just over the hill, but I choose not to do any more exploring. Instead I pedal back to my campsite.

I listen to the noisy sounds generated from the town and surrounding area, and decide to take the neighbor's earlier suggestion and ignore the lively echo. There are no bathing facilities at the campground so I will have to wait until tomorrow for the $1 shower at the harbor. When silence takes over the night, I can finally reflect on my day. I realize that the forty miles I have traveled today is the farthest I have pedaled in the last week because of all the incredible sights I stopped to explore along the way. I marvel at the affordable transportation options on these Islands, but smile when I glance over to my bike and realize how lucky I am to be afforded the time, good health and resources to engage in this extended gap from everyday life.

I wake up with a dream still sharp and clear in my mind. Moe and I are pedaling together on a tandem bicycle along a coastal road and stop to go for a swim in the warm turquoise waters. The sun is low in the western sky and the full moon is starting to rise as we emerge from the sea. This is a beautiful way to start my day as I wonder just what beach we might have been visiting.

As I prepare to leave the campground, I glance up and notice that the sun is peeking out from time to time behind the billowy clouds. The five-mile ride, past a golf course retirement community, to Vesuvius, a one-street town with an inn, store, restaurant and the ferry terminal, is quick and uneventful. For the first time on my journey, I ride right onto the ferry, without having to wait The next island, Crofton, is only a ten-minute ferry ride away and I see many smoke stacks indicating there is a very large timber mill near by. As we head into the harbor, we maneuver past large quantities of gigantic logs, pulp and shavings being transported on, or attached to the back of barges as they float to their destination.

Since there is no reason to linger in this industrial area, I take off on a two-lane road winding through old growth forests for fifteen miles. The pine trees, fifteen to twenty feet tall, dwarf my image as I soar through the area. Amongst the tiny farms, the colorful town of Chemainus emerges. Large, brilliantly detailed murals (thirty-seven in all), depicting the history of the community, have been painted on buildings, fences and literally any strategically placed surface to create a tourist attraction which fills the economic gap when the mills are closed. The vision of the town fathers did wonders in reinventing and rejuvenating this island town.

I had to park my bike, grab a walking tour map and follow the yellow footsteps around town in order to relive the history of this area, depicted in the murals. I could not help but notice all the stylish boutiques, unique bistros, art galleries and the dinner theater building. This makes a great destination for tourists wanting to experience a fun weekend get-away or just a whistle-stop for those, like myself, who are on an extended tour of the Islands. The railroads, an important part of the timber industry's history, still operate on the Salt Spring Island, providing another transportation venue for tourists traveling in this area. I decide to forgo the tour of the working sawmill and get back on the road.

I notice that retirement homes, sometimes referred to as 'patio living', are being promoted in this area. As a flip side of this concept, I see a sign indicating I can bungee jump off one of the bridges in Nanaimo. Neither option appeals to me at the moment so I merge onto Highway #1 and am immediately overwhelmed by the offensive noise of truck traffic. The exit to Nanaimo comes none too soon, and I am delighted to be away from the chaos and in the warm flow of another harbor-side shower. I find a spot for lunch and stop to talk to a few truck drivers who are eating at the next table. They tell me that there is a lot of road construction on the highway going north. Without a second thought, I find myself heading toward the ferry dock.

As I stare at the ferry schedule and maps, I contemplate my choices. The ferry going south to Twsawassen is leaving now, 3:30 p.m.; the one heading west, to Vancouver, leaves at 5 p.m. It is a two-hour trip either way, but when another biker, with whom I converse, tells me of a camping area next to a water park near the ferry landing in Twsawassen, I decide on the first option. Now that I have a plan, I am able to settle in for the ride and watch the island mounds in the distance surrounded by the deep blue sea. My timing could not be more perfect. I am able to find the campground and assemble my tent by 6:15 p.m. just as the sun is going down in the west. I have gotten this process down to a science and can do the entire job in seven minutes. Not only is the water park closing for the season, but the little grocery store is clearing its shelves and all I can find for dinner is a jar of dill pickles. Perhaps this is not the strangest dinner I have ever had, but it ranks close.

I lie awake planning my next destination and recall my friend Paul's seventieth birthday party in Vail where I first heard about Jack from Vancouver. I was impressed that so many people from Paul's youth through the present time came from such distances to celebrate his birthday or sent memories via video. They each had a story to tell about the youthful senior.

Jack, unable to attend, sent his story by messenger. He recalled the story from their youth when he and Paul used to drive, almost every weekend, from Toronto to Mount Trenblant, where they skied hard and partied harder. They always made a plan to be on the road on Sunday by 3 p.m., but repeatedly seemed to end up in a bar at that hour rather than behind the wheel of their car. It was sometimes close to mid-night by the time they actually departed the ski area and began their seven-hour drive home. Well, one time they found themselves in the midst of a heavy snowstorm and were both so wiped-out that they had to keep switching drivers, sometimes as often as every ten minutes! Finally, they could go no further and decided to check into a motel for the remainder of the night. In the morning, they discovered they were only twenty-five miles from home.

At a later party at Paul's house, we called Jack and Monica on the phone so that Paul could introduce me and let them know that I would soon be traveling in British Columbia and would like to stop by and meet them.

I guess it is ok to be self-centered when I am traveling alone, but my mind wanders back to memories of my fortieth birthday party. I decided to throw myself a bash. I needed a location, something different, not the usual club or restaurant. My good friend, Kahuna, was living at Ski Patrol Headquarters on top of the mountain next to chair four so I decided to pay him a visit. He thought it would be fine to use the deck and apartment and set up a buffet on the private outdoor area behind the apartment. The next item on my agenda was to find a caterer who could create an interesting assortment of foods, and be able to deliver the food to the top of the mountain at the specified time. Again, I relied on an old friend to help. We worked out a menu and the food was prepared, delivered and set-up on the big day. The details of the party got out, as it always did in Vail, by word of mouth. The early spring weather could not have been more perfect for the sixth day of February. Under a Colorado-blue sky and mild temperatures, crowds showed up at Patrol Headquarters; some only for a quick beer between ski runs and others lingered until the chair lifts closed and took advantage of the food adorning the table, the beverages that flowed and the drugs that were not-too- discretely available. As the sun began to set, the last of the guests, who still had the ability to ski down the mountain, slid away. But, the party was not quite over! Kahuna told me to stay put, and he would come back shortly with my birthday present. He vanished in his snow mobile after dark, returning a short time later with one of the waitresses from the club I was managing. The next morning at 6 a.m., before the mountain crew showed up for work, Kahuna drove both the young lady and me down the mountain on the snow mobile. I tucked the cheerful memories of my birthday inside my mind and began the fortieth year of my life. A week later, I wanted to go skiing, but could not find my skies. It took me the whole day to realize that I had left them at Patrol Headquarters the day of the party since I was driven down the mountain on a snow mobile.

Jack and his wife, Monica, live in a suburb of North Vancouver. They invited me to stay for a week and come and go as I please with a, "The key is under the mat." This is an offer I cannot turn down and sleeping indoors on a soft bed with a shower and laundry facilities nearby will be a welcome change from the star-studded hotels in which I have been spending my nights during my last few weeks on the road.

I awake to another dew-drenched day which rapidly becomes a clear, sunny fifty-eight degrees. I stretch my tent and sleeping bag out on the picnic table next to my wooden platform and talk to my neighbors as I am waiting for my gear to dry. They share some important information concerning my plan for entering the city. I am forced to reroute because of a construction project which will add ten miles to the trip. The terrain is delta land; a flat and low surface which once arose from the river dropping collected soil which eroded upstream. Today, it has been developed by the wealthy into pristine farms and homes. I turn onto a two-lane road with a bike path sixty percent of the way and find it takes me right to where I want to go. I cross the first of four bridges and glance down at the tugboats bringing logs down to the mills. I stop off and on to take some amazing photos of two tugboats playing bumper cars with each other and another set of pictures of a seaplane taking flight over a bridge as a freighter goes under the same bridge simultaneously.

The city is covered in a blanket of fog which finally clears up around 1 p.m. Vancouver, a city surrounded by water on three sides, sits in a valley with inlets running through it like rivers. It is snuggled against a snow-mantled mountain range with a ski area just outside North Vancouver where I am headed. I pass a park, then Chinatown and ride along the waterfront before I realize that the last five miles of my trip to Jack and Monica's house will be all uphill. I take it with spirit and know I will be sipping a cold beer in front of a television within the hour and, yes, the key is under the mat!

Monica returns from work and lets me know that Jack is on a sales trip in the interior and will return in a few days but that does not stop her from welcoming me to their home and neighborhood. We set out for dinner at a local pub and share stories of our lives. I am surprised when Monica comments how she would like to trade places with me. I guess I do not fully realize the uniqueness of this adventure and my whole life.

For the first time in weeks, I don't wake up in a paradise of dampness and, not surprisingly, find it a bit more difficult to get out of this soft, warm bed than it was to step foot out of my sleeping bag. Remembering from yesterday's ride that the city of Vancouver is enshrouded in a fog till mid-morning, I take my time and browse through a few of Monica and Jack's books on the city and surrounding area.

I walk the couple of miles downhill and catch a ferry for less than $2. In fifteen minutes I am in downtown Vancouver. As I glance at the water surrounding me, I am not surprised that this is the largest seaport in British Colombia. When I step off the ferry, I am in a cosmopolitan city which offers all the urban amenities I could ever need. I glance upward and around as far as my eyes can see and I notice the contrast of heritage and modern architecture. I am most interested in seeing Gastown, the city's oldest neighborhood which turns out to be nothing more than a very popular shopping Mecca.

Next, I head over to #1 Canada Place to take a look at the interesting multi-level building with billowy sails covering a courtyard which hugs the waterfront. I am told that if all the buildings with modern blue glass were removed from the downtown area, you would be looking at the skyline that was once visible three to four years ago. The many sailboats moored in the quays near the edge of the city shout adventure and fun to me.

By this time, I have my fill of concrete and head to Stanley Park. I am excited when I see that you can bike or ride the seawall all the way around the park and west for miles to the University of British Colombia. I am beginning to formulate a plan for tomorrow which will include my bike.

As I scout the many trails leading in all directions, I am awestruck. If you could see the vastness of this city park in proportion to the downtown area from the sky, you would better understand the respect the forefathers had for this land. In 1939, a reporter from *The News Herald* was able to put these feelings into words: "A city that has been carved out of the forest should maintain, somewhere within its boundaries, evidence of what it once was." The giant trees that fill Stanley Park proclaim the story of Vancouver's infancy.

The park and all the green spaces and city streets in Vancouver are spotless. There are no homeless people to be seen. I can easily see why Vancouver is a very pricey place to live. In fact, the prices in the real estate market are second only to Los Angeles.

My watch tells me it is time to head back to #1 Canada Place to meet an old acquaintance from my past in Vail. Michelle recognizes me right away and, frankly, lets me know that her memories of me are a bit tarnished. She and I were acquainted during the days when my life in Vail and Aspen were consumed with sex, drugs and rock 'n roll. We talked for several hours and she can see that I am a changed man and would be an acceptable guest to invite to dinner and meet a few friends at her house tomorrow night. I tell her that I will be riding my bicycle to her house, and she invites me to spend the night.

I am a bit hyped up after a few cups of coffee and wish I had my bike to work off some of this caffeine, but the City bus will have to do and it is right at the curb waiting for me. I decide to go to Granville Island to explore this refurbished neighborhood. It was once an industrial park that was transformed into a touristy spot with interesting shops and trendy restaurants mixed in with an old functioning cement plant and several shipyard businesses. My footsteps lead me from one shop to the next before I head back to the big city to catch a ferry to North Vancouver where I am planning to meet Monica for dinner at the house.

Once again on my journey, I am able to impress someone with a respectable outfit pulled out of my panniers that include jeans and cowboy boots.

It seems that I will never tire of being served salmon, a west coast specialty, or of hearing stories of life on the road. Jack calls and assures me that he still lives at the house and will be home in a couple more days. I share my plans for tomorrow with Monica and she gives me a few pointers of things not to miss along the way. We both are tired from the day, and I am happy to plop down on my luxurious bed and do a little more reading about the surrounding area. Before long, I close my eyes and don't open them until the next morning.

I pack a few things in my panniers for my night at Michelle's place and hop on my bike for what I anticipate to be a long ride. Once I am across the water by ferry and am once again in Vancouver, I head straight to Stanley Park. I find the bike path without getting lost. and ride out in beautiful weather. I am surprised that I only cover thirty miles in three hours. The scenic path and my casual pace afford me glimpses along the way of the Rowing Club, The National Geographic Tree, the geodesic dome at the Science Center, the amazing natural rock formation known as Siwash Rock, all three beaches, Brockton viewpoint and an assortment of plaques and statues including Girl in Wet Suit, which sits out in the bay.

When I reach the Totem Park, I stop to admire these giant sculptures and take a few photos to show Moe. The park within a park is situated just off the seawall beside the Brockton Oval cricket pitch. There are eight totem poles; each tells a story that breathes life into it. The small interpretive center with a gift shop houses displays that describe how the Northwest Coast First Nations came to create these wonders of the art world. The towering Cascade Mountains, as the background, make a most impressive backdrop for these carved cedar sculptures of animals and supernatural beings that honor the First Nations of Stanley Park.

I ride through the University of British Columbia campus, which is dotted with some very old, stately-looking buildings. The UBC grounds are spread out over a large piece of land at the western point of Vancouver. I glance at all the students hustling back and forth to classes, chatting, carrying backpacks and, of course, cell phones. I regret that I never had this friendly learning experience in my early twenties. The draft was being enforced in 1965 and that guided my direction into the US Army.

Luckily, I was not sent to Viet Nam; instead I was stationed in Colorado Springs at Ft. Carson. I kept my hair as long as possible so that I could try and pass for a college student. I often ventured onto the campus at Colorado College and attempted to mix in with the students. I found it very hard listening to students condemning soldiers, like myself, for their part in the war effort. It wasn't like I wanted to be in the Army, but at that time, I had very few choices. The students were always able to figure out that I was a soldier and let me know I did not belong. There was never room for discussion. It was a sad time for our generation; but after my term served in the Army, I made up for lost time.

The bike path weaves in and out of neighborhoods and I stop along the way to enjoy the parks and scenic places or other points of interest. In one of the parks, I see two huge swimming pools almost twice the size of the Glenwood Hot Springs pools in Colorado. These Vancouver city pools are water-fed from the river and then purified. They are an example of some of the publicly funded facilities in and around this fabulous city.

I arrive at Michelle's place at 5 p.m. and find her entertaining a couple of friends who have stopped to say 'Hi'. We share a bottle of wine and Linda and Colby invite us up to Whistler for dinner at their condo on Sunday. This is a perfect opportunity for me to see another part of the area. After they leave, Michelle and I have a nice chicken dinner and a couple more glasses of wine and take turns launching into one story after the next. I spend the night on the couch and awake to a splash of color and blinding sunlight streaming in the living room window.

Michelle makes coffee and a light breakfast. She needs to get to work, so I head off on my bike back to town via the Harbor View Tower building where I am able to take a ride up the elevator to a viewing deck to take more photos of the city. I am spellbound once again by the power of the landscape. I depart and hop on my bicycle and continue to explore Stanley Park, including the fish hatchery.

Before returning to Jack and Monica's house, I ride up to Grouse Mountain Ski Area just beyond their house. Grouse Mountain has two trams and is only about ten minutes by car from the house. The ride up the tram will cost $17 so I pass and take in the view from ground level. It is easy to see that the city has grown to its doorstep. The weather remains pleasant as the day goes on and the riding is great.

I arrive at the house and find that Jack is finally home. They have plans to go to a friend's place for dinner and I am invited. We stop to pick up three bottles of wine on the way over so I know we are in for another rough night and, of course, salmon is the entrée for the evening. We have a nice time and head home for more cocktails in front of the fireplace with its flickering and sputtering flames. In our enlightened state, we decide to give Paul Caldwell a wake-up call at 3 a.m in Colorado. He is not delighted with the timing of our call, so we say our good-byes and head to bed.

On Sunday morning, Michelle picks me up at 10 a.m. and we head up to Whistler and Blackcomb ski areas. The seventy-two-mile drive up takes one and a half hours and is one of the most beautiful drives I have ever experienced. The Sea to Sky Corridor of British Columbia is sometimes referred to as Hell's Highway. This nickname describes its dangerous curves which that have taken the lives of nine people so far this year. The mountains, glaciers, lakes and ocean along the way make every turn in the road a spectacular vista. I can't take my eyes off the landscape and am torn between focusing on the secluded sandy beaches far below, the pine-scented forest with its ancient trees or the snow blanketing the mountain tops stretching to the sky. The road is narrow in areas and traffic moves quite fast so pulling over for pictures is not in the cards. We arrive at the ski area at the same time the Whistler Mountaineer Train pulls into the station. I make a mental note of this transportation option. The journey from the city takes three hours with the train hugging the oceanfront, winding through canyons and climbing the steep grades of the British Columbia Coast Mountains as it offers a unique perspective of the breathtaking views.

In spite of the fact that the ski areas and towns of Whistler and Blackcomb are side by side, they have separate ownership and are independent. The ski tickets for exploring the 8,000 acres of terrain are interchangeable and the two towns compete for customers. An old friend, Terry Minger, one of Vail, Colorado's past town managers, helped in the town's planning stages. The area reminds me somewhat of Beaver Creek, Vail's neighboring ski area, because the walking village is wide and restaurants spill over into the malls. There are hiking trails galore and some are lit up at night. Lost Lake, with sunning decks and beaches, is near the heart of the core area of these two beautiful towns. I am told it is heavily used in the summer, along with the two signature golf courses which complete the picture.

We stop at an open house and find out that property sells for about $300 a square foot. We play tourist and wander in and out of shops along the mall before heading just up the road from the village to have dinner at Linda and Colby's condo. Along the way we see prestigious private homes sitting up on a rocky abutment overlooking the golf course and lake with views of the ski area and mountains. Linda and Colby's house has some of those same spectacular views.

Again, salmon is the entrée, but only one bottle of wine is corked; Michelle is most grateful, as her friends know, she will have to face a treacherous highway drive down the mountain soon after dinner. We have a great time, and I am invited up for skiing this winter if I am interested. As the sun is setting in the west, we head back home along the scenic highway which seems to flow from the sky to the sea. Michelle and I have had a great time renewing our friendship and she invites me to visit anytime. As I close my eyes, I realize that I long for the companionship and deeper feelings that Moe and I were steadily building while we were in Vail together. I need to find a way to put into words what I am feeling towards Moe, but for now, I am on a journey of a lifetime and will focus on each experience that comes my way.

On Monday, I try to get an early start because I have a forty-mile ride to catch the 11 a.m. ferry to Vancouver Island where I will catch a 3 p.m. boat out of Victoria to Port Angeles. If I don't arrive on time for the 11 a.m. ferry, there is another one scheduled at 1 p.m., but I will miss my 3 p.m. connection. With a stroke of luck, all goes as planned and I reach Swartz Bay on Vancouver Island at 2:45 p.m. I am confident that I remember the way along the back roads to Victoria as this is my second stop at Swartz Bay. The ride is an easy glide into Thetis Lake Campground.

After cleaning up, I walk down the highway a half-mile to a local fish 'n chips place for an inexpensive dinner then back up to Thetis Lake to watch the sun set. The purple color tinting the clouds reflects off the lake and the surroundings are peaceful and beautiful. The night is uneventful; I fade off to sleep in my cozy little cocoon. I awake at 7 a.m. to a cold forty degrees and put on some extra clothes for the short ride to downtown inner harbor where I board the Coho Ferry to Port Angeles. I exchange my last $40 Canadian and get $30 US dollars.

twelve

Today is Oct. 4th and, to my surprise at 10 a.m. I am already stripping down to shorts and a short sleeve shirt. There is not a cloud in the sky, but the weather report indicates that a change will take place soon. I would like to come back sometime and ride the sunshine coast of Vancouver Island further north and visit Tofino and the Pacific Rim National Park on the west coast. The national park is backed by the Insular Mountain Range of Vancouver Island and faces the open Pacific Ocean. It has a cool and wet maritime climate producing an abundance of life in the water and on land. Besides the natural wonders, the area offers glimpses into the long and dynamic history of the Nuu-chah-nulth First Nations and European explorers and settlers. I know that Moe would love to do some hiking along the West Coast Trail.

I seem to have hit a wall, and am starting to feel a bit run down for the first time on my journey. The ferry to Port Angeles is on time and I, tentatively, step aboard and am filled with a sense of relief that I have at least one and a half hours to rest and hopefully feel rejuvenated when the boat arrives in Port Angeles. I shield my eyes from the glare and am painfully aware that I am now traveling with one less possession, a pair of sunglasses.

When the ferryboat finally nudges along the side of the dock, I confidently walk my bike down the dock and am on the road by 12:30 p.m. I was hoping to stop in Port Townsend along the way, but it is thirteen miles off the highway I am traveling on and I am trying to make it to Jackie's house before sunset. I have become spoiled pedaling on quiet country roads without the imposing presence of ten-wheelers and noisy cars. In spite of the lack of ambiance, the road has a very wide shoulder and is easy to navigate the whole way to Highway # 104.

On my right, I have a view of the Olympia Mountain Range, which to my surprise is thickly covered with pine trees. It is quite hilly, rather than rocky and snow-peaked as I had expected. On my left is the ocean and snow-capped Mt. Baker looms in the distance. Highway # 104 quickly becomes hilly with many long uphill stretches. My knee starts hurting at the fifty-mile mark and I stop to wrap it with an Ace bandage. I suspected that I might need this at some time along the way and feel quite happy that I am on one of the last segments of my journey when I have to pull it out from the bottom of my panniers and put it on. The knee becomes weaker as the day wears on and I find myself pedaling with only the force of my right leg.

I am on my way to visit Jackie Flater Wood, her husband, Rich, and their two children on Bainbridge Island. She was a good friend of mine in Vail. I have known Rich's brother for years, but only met Rich once or twice. I have called them along the way and they seem very excited that I am coming to visit.

The same pattern of my mind, drifting backwards to a time in Vail or Aspen when I was younger, emerged about this colorful family. Jackie and Rich were getting married and I wanted to make a contribution to the celebration that was spread out over a week. The bachelorette party was taking place at Jackie's mom's condo at the Vorlaufer in Vail Village, where she lived at the time. I was getting myself sufficiently liquored and pulled out a book of artistic body painting that I had received for my birthday. I decided to paint my body, highlighting certain areas in silver and black. When the creation was finished, I covered my artwork with a towel and jacket and walked one hundred yards to the scene of the party, but, not surprisingly, lost my nerve along the way. I decided it was not such a great idea after all and quickly walked back home praying I would not be seen by any of my neighbors.

Now, talk about dressing funny - Rich's brother, Rusty, who worked for me as a bartender at the Bridge Street Shuffle, decided to come to work one winter evening wearing a red chiffon dress. He proceeded to pour cocktails throughout the night as if there was nothing unusual about the scene. I had a feeling that if Rusty could pull off this type of prank, his brother must have other interesting tales to tell about when they were growing up together.

The story juices are starting to really flow as I am riding my bike along and thinking about the strange happenings of my past. Suddenly, out of that place in my brain that stores these memories, pops the strangest story of them all. It was January, 1969, when my sister, Louisa, decided to visit me in Vail. It happened to be Airline Week which was a marketing scheme Vail used to increase business during the slow month of January. The event *du jour* was a bikini contest between the airline stews and the girls of Vail. Well, my sister got caught up in the event so I introduced her to my friend Lee Caracelli, who agreed to help preen her for the event. She shaved and plucked unwanted hair, manicured and pedicured the nails, applied make-up and donned a blond bouffant wig; but the stroke of luck was that the white leather bikini that belonged to Lee was a perfect fit! Together we headed off to the Villa Valhalla pool where the event was to take place. Some of you may have guessed because of the extensive hair removal task that the new Queen of Vail was none other than me. By the time the crowns were handed out and photos taken, I realized that I was late for work. I rushed off to the Clock Tower Bar where I worked as a bartender-in-training. There was no time to change into my uniform, and when the bar manager saw me he told the owner, John Kaemmer, that if he did not make me leave he would quit. John, having a wonderful sense of humor, said that the bar manager could leave anytime and he did. I remained behind the bar, clad in my white leather bikini until last call! That's enough about cross-dressing, at least for now.

My spirits are a little down as I start to realize that I may not be able to reach Jackie and Rich's house before sunset. I am feeling the cool fresh air against my face and I suddenly recognize that I am at the Hood Canal Bridge and know I only have another twenty miles to go. I don't have to take out a map to also know that, since I am on an island, I should expect these twenty miles to include more uphill terrain than down.

The coastal beaches, with only a dozen seagulls squatting on the sand and the mesmerizing ocean waves gently lapping on the shore, calm my nerves and bring me back to the importance of experiencing only this moment in time, rather than worrying what the next nineteen and a half miles might have in store for me.

I vigorously pedal across the bridge to Bainbridge Island just as a few loitering shadows begin to appear on the highway. I have another four to five miles to go and do not want to give in to the looming fear that it will be too dark, too soon. I am thankful that the shoulder of the road remains wide as I reach the final two turns on the highway. I take a left onto a small secondary road with farms and homes filling in the landscape. I am not prepared for the fact that the road that Jackie lives on is not marked, but I follow my instinct and turn to look down the street and there, four houses down is the white fence I had hoped to find.

A modern, gray wooden two-story house with white trim was built across the yard from the old farmhouse that they had purchased and originally lived in during the construction phase. The five-acre property has a barn, complete with horses and is screened with trees for privacy. Jackie and Rich are waiting in the living room and getting ready to prepare, you guessed it, salmon pasta. I am not even aware of being hungry, as the opportunity to relax with a glass of wine in the company of old friends is most satisfying. They escort me to the guest room and tell me to take my time cleaning up and we will have dinner when I am ready. The children have already eaten and are busy with homework and catching a favorite TV show before retiring to their rooms. We finish a bottle of wine over dinner which evolves into dessert and after-dinner drinks while telling stories of past travels and our memories of the early days of Vail. Jackie has never heard the story about her bachelorette party and the black and silver guest who never arrived and we got a good chuckle over that one.

They both thank me for the wedding gift of a limo. I was in the transportation business at the time and only recall scattered things about their wedding. I instantly feel better knowing that I did make some special contribution to the event after all.

While sharing stories from my bike trip and my recent visit with Kirk Reinike, Jackie tells me that she was at Steamboat Springs, Colorado, racing for Ski Club Vail the weekend I replaced the coach who had been injured in a car accident as the skiers chaperon and stand-in coach. Small world!

They tell me that I am welcome to stay as long as I want in the old farmhouse, and they aren't talking days. I had not expected this opportunity to arise, but will take it into serious consideration. While settling into a warm, soft bed, I congratulate myself on the fact that I managed to travel ninety-four miles today, only five of which were before 12:30 p.m.

I wake up the next day and say good-bye to the family taking off in different directions for work and school. I decide to ride my bike around Bainbridge Island to try to locate the town center. I have a good introduction to fall weather in the islands off Puget Sound. The day starts off with clear, blue skies and a cool thirty-eight degrees and steadily warms to seventy-five before a cloud cover comes in and temperatures drop to sixty. An elderly gentleman sitting in front of a small store tells me that a front is supposed to move through tonight.

I am thinking about Jackie and Rich's offer that they presented last night as I pick up the local paper and look through the help-wanted section. I find a few jobs at $7 to $8.50 an hour, which do not interest me in the least. There is one ad for a handy man that intrigues me. I place a call and find out that he charges $20 an hour and is ready to come out and do any work I need; in other words, he is not very busy. Job prospects on the island are not too promising so perhaps this is a sign?

The town center by the ferry is composed of a few blocks and I note that Bainbridge is advertised as a historic town. I find its link to days gone by with a 100-year-old church, but disappointedly, am not able to find much of a restored historical commercial district. There are a few trendy cafes and one-of-a-kind island souvenir shops in Winslow, but I do take the time to browse.

I pedal over to the library to check out the progress of my stocks in the *Wall Street Journal* and the news is not exhilarating. I continue my tour of the Island, which has fifty-three miles of shoreline, five miles wide and ten miles long. I head back to the house and when the maid arrives, I take a walk around the neighborhood and enjoy the peaceful surroundings of small farms and homes on large tracks of land.

The kids join us for a shrimp pasta dinner at home and I make the Clock Tower's famous Caesar salad to accompany the meal. I can tell that having visitors during the workweek is a bit disruptive to the family and I am not a bit offended when they suggest an early retirement.

I am awakened by the sound of pots and pans clattering in the kitchen and become suddenly fascinated watching the light dancing across the walls in the room. It is interesting to have the time to wake up so casually in such comforting surroundings. My mind quickly moves backward and I think about why I have to always be trying so hard to understand my past. I thought this was something someone does when he is in the last stages of life. Maybe this is the purpose of my bicycle trip? Maybe I will be able to make peace with the past and be ready for what the future presents. Today I will go with the flow, as Jackie has taken the day off from work to show me her favorite spots on the Island.

I join her in the kitchen and, together, we work on a few chores that need to be done around the house before going on a tour by car, in what appears at the moment to be a beautiful, sun-struck day. We start with the old farmhouse where they first lived when they came to Bainbridge Island. What a contrast it is to their elegant new house. The tour continues to the golf club which is open most of the year, but no one is visible on the course. I remember that Jackie and I used to participate in the famous No Name Golf Tournament in Vail and that there is a photo of her in a golf cart at the tournament on the wall at Bart & Yeti's restaurant where she worked as a waitress during breaks from law school. Our next stop is the general store and a few other shops where we pick up some sea bass for dinner and head home along the gently curving road that leads away from the placid waters of the sound.

Jackie shows me around the barn and horse-training area, as well as the tack room with several English saddles and all the gear to go with them. She introduces me to her new horse and lets me know that she is in the process of training him for show. She saddles him up and begins his training session in the ring. From the size of the ring, barn and tack, I conclude that this is obviously more than a passing hobby.

I sit on the fence near the tack room and begin to recall the summer of 1970 when rodeo nights were set up at the East Vail Ranch. Locals like Gordie Rowe, Chupa Nelson, John English and Ron Riley would round up other locals to basically put on a show on Friday nights for the tourists. The owner of the ranch would supply the horses, along with a few bulls brought in from Eagle and, sometimes, there were even a few bucking broncos. Not surprisingly, the rodeo events also became a venue to wager on. A friend of John's from Boston, Louie Banana, who went by this alias because the mob was looking for him to settle a few bad wagers, became the bookie. He figured out a way to handicap the events and took all bets. Of course, I had to get involved and tried my luck on a bucking bronco.

After watching and photographing Jackie as she goes through a few maneuvers with her horse, I retire to the house. I am happy to be able to take advantage of this little window of time and spend it reading about the area. I jot down a few notes to go over with Rich and Jackie and am ready to begin to make a plan for what I want to see in the upcoming days.

The following morning, I take my bike to the shop to have my wheel trued and a broken spoke repaired. Jason, the mechanic who is going to work on my bike, kindly gives me a ride to the ferry so I can go into the city of Seattle. I casually board a large ferry under pale blue skies, now scattered with clouds. The thirty-five-minute ride gives me some perspective as to the fact that forty-one percent of the city limits is made up of water. I am fascinated with the variety of seagoing vessels, such as tugboats, barges, commercial fishing boats and pleasure crafts that we pass on the way to the downtown harbor.

My walking tour of Seattle begins at the wharf where all the tourist restaurants and shops are located. I stop at the Omni-Max Theater and catch the movie about Mount St. Helens on the big bubble (fish-eye) screen. The top of the mountain came barreling down after a massive eruption on the morning of May 18, 1980. I try to imagine what it might have been like to be among the thousands whose lives were disrupted on that morning and how 200-square-miles of rich forest was changed into a grey, lifeless landscape. Time is helping to heal the land, but I had not planned to ride near the disaster site on this trip since my footsteps would instead be taking me south along the coast from Seattle. The images displayed in the movie fascinate me, and my respect for the power and unpredictability of Mother Nature has once again been renewed.

Stiff muscles from sitting a good part of the morning encourage me to get my body moving so I head over to the famous Pike Street Market. The market boasts that it is the oldest continuously operating farmers' market in the United States. This huge four or five-story, block-wide warehouse stretches along several blocks and is filled with shops and eateries. It is obviously much more than a place where farmers sell their produce. I am not ready for the sensory overload coming from the smells of the fish section of the market and quickly take note that one would need a couple of days to tour the entire place. I find it too crowded and uncomfortable to continue so I head into the city where I catch a monorail for a mile ride to Seattle Center.

This is the site of the 1962 World's Fair, with the Space Needle being its signature structure. I pay the $6.50 to go on my skyward journey 605 feet into the air. The 360-degree views are spectacular. I am actually able to see some of the 150 bridges crossing the city waterways, the Olympic and Cascade Mountain Ranges, Mt. Rainier and Puget Sound dotted with miniature boats. I am told that the city of Seattle is also called the Emerald City and the many patches of green are a striking contrast against the deep blue-green water. I take a few pictures and then head back down and into town on the monorail.

I walk over to the sixty-story office building where Jackie works as an attorney and go up to the forty-third floor where the view is almost better than the Space Needle. Jackie ties up some loose ends at work and then takes me to Pioneer Square the original downtown section of Seattle. Six blocks of restored century-old buildings, many of them influenced by Victorian and Romanesque architecture, have been converted to restaurants, shops, offices, nightclubs and art galleries. A small tower, completed in 1914, overlooking the square is recorded to have been the tallest building west of the Mississippi, once upon a time. We stroll among the crowd engrossed in conversations of their own. I notice that there are even weirder, homeless characters pan-handling in Pioneer Square than in other parts of the city I have explored. We step onto one of the cars on the old streetcar system still in use. It has been refurbished and operates in tourist areas of the city. We stop for a cocktail at a New Orleans jazz club then coffee at a bookstore before catching a ferry home. At the terminal we meet Rich and his boss and we all ride back together.

Rich generously offers to go home and take care of the kids while

Jackie finishes taking me on the royal tour. We stop at a pub on the waterfront and she shows me Ross Davis' (mutual friend from Vail) worn-out boat. She mentions that I can live on it, but it is in such bad shape that I wouldn't consider it. The condition of Ross' boat all too plainly reminds me of my last experience on a sailboat which left more than a salty taste in my mouth. Our last stop is a restaurant called the Four Swallows, located in an old house. The ambiance far surpasses the quality of food offered on the menu, but in all fairness, we only have an appetizer and head home.

That night, as I was driving home with Jackie, I told her the story of what happened when I was part of a crew on *the sail boat from hell.* When I was traveling in Central America, I met a man in Costa Rica who had a fifty-five foot sailboat he had been sailing around the world. He had just finished the Caribbean racing circuit and was not interested in any more sea-time. After a drink together, he asked if I would stay on his boat in Gulfito and guard it until the crew arrived from San Francisco. He let me know that I was welcome to join them and experience a Pacific sailing journey.

Two weeks later, the crew found me at the yacht club and the Captain announced that he wanted to leave at daybreak. The first thing I noticed about the crew was that they were all over six feet, four inches tall and the captain was a Maori from New Zealand. At our introductory meeting, he and the navigator tell me that they have raced together in the America's Cup on Ted Turner's crew. I was impressed and felt like we would be in good hands. We discussed our departure scheduled for early the next morning. The Captain said we would sail twenty-four hours a day straight and rotate four-hour, on-again-off-again shifts. He announced that there would be no drinking on the voyage, and that our arrival in San Francisco was scheduled for two weeks from tomorrow.

I knew there was a problem from the start when the Captain tried to pull up the mooring. Even when I told him it was a mooring, not an anchor, he kept trying to tug at it unsuccessfully. After twenty minutes, the Harbor Master came on our radio and said to the Captain, "That mooring is in pretty good isn't it?" Embarrassed, the Captain dropped the line and motored away from the harbor amidst snickering comments from the crowd that had gathered on the dock. This would not be the last time we'd be laughed at on our trip! Six hours later we arrived in Puntarenas. The Captain wanted to clear immigration so he and the navigator went ashore and left the first mate and me stranded on board without a dingy or passports. Several hours later, we got a ride to shore and we were able to find our Captain and navigator at the nearest bar, half in the bag. So much for the first rule - *no drinking until we reach San Francisco* - a rule the Captain set down before we departed on the trip.

A few hours later we motored out to sea and were boarded by the Costa Rican Coast Guard for no apparent reason other than it probably looked suspicious to be heading out to sea that late in the evening with a storm approaching. They held us outside on deck in an incredible downpour guarded by two machine-gun-toting soldiers while the commandant and his buddy ransacked the boat looking for booty. They found nothing, so they just departed and let us go on our way without a comment. By mid-morning, we had reached the resort community of Flamingos in the northwest part of the country. The Captain said we'd be there a few hours to take on water and fuel. After filling up, we moved away from the dock and anchored. Again the Captain and the navigator went ashore in the dingy to investigate the surroundings and make further purchases. Several hours later, the first mate and I again hitched a ride to shore. This time we found them, you guessed it, in a bar. We returned to the boat and prepared to depart, but the Captain did not take into account that we had anchored at high tide. Now, with the additional weight of the water and fuel, the boat's fifteen-foot keel and the presence of low tide, we found ourselves dragging the bottom as we tried to motor away. Again a crowd was forming on the dock as the Captain tried to solve the problem by hiring two forty-foot sport fishing boats to throw a line out to the stern and another to the bow to pull us around in a circle as we augured deeper and deeper into the sandy bottom. They finally stopped when part of the stern on one of the boats actually ripped off. We had no choice but to wait for the tide to rise so that we could sail out. Once we were free, we motored out and anchored offshore. To my amazement, the Captain was not embarrassed to show his face in town so all of us boarded the dingy and went ashore for dinner. With the announced tight schedule in mind, the Captain changed his mind and decided to party for four days. When we finally sailed out, we did cover some territory along the Pacific coast, but unfortunately we were bearing down on Acapulco. It was like *déjà vu* to me as I watched the Captain and the navigator motor into the port in the dingy. Once again, the first mate and I remained behind. We were getting quite good at hitchhiking into shore and finding our leaders drinking shots of tequila at another bar.

This time the excuse for delaying our voyage had to do with a recent misadventure at sea. A few nights before, at 2 a.m. we found ourselves approaching stormy weather detected by the radar, but ignored by the Captain. He made the decision to go through the storm, rather than around it. By midnight, we found ourselves trying to reef the mainsail in the middle of the Pacific Ocean in the midst of violent winds. This choice led to a fifteen-foot rip right down the middle of the mainsail. Four or five days later the repair was made and the Captain caught me trying to jump ship just before we left Acapulco. I reluctantly stayed on board as we motored out under sunny skies, wondering what else was in store for us on our journey north.

Using the excuse that Hurricane Eduardo was blowing in, the captain decided that Cabo San Lucas would be our next port of entry. The dingy motor and the reverse gear on the sailboat were no longer working so the Captain was forced to pull up to the dock. We went into town to spend the night. Five days later, with a belly full of tequila and rum, the Captain summoned us back to the boat for the last leg of our journey. He had spent all his money partying in town so there was no money left for food or ice.

Word was sent to us that the owner of the boat wanted us to dock in San Diego rather than sail up to San Francisco. He had heard rumors of our escapades in the Pacific coast towns from Gulfito north. There was still a bottle of rum and the owner's champagne on board, but, somehow, it managed to disappear before we motored into the San Diego Yacht Club. The Captain's wife, rather than the owner, was waiting with money to pay the crew. The owner was not ready to see the remains of what happened to his boat under the irresponsible leadership of our Captain. I was paid half of what I was promised for what turned out to be a six-week journey, rather than the planned two week sail... That would be my last sailing adventure for a while.

Jackie glances over and gives me a surprised look and says she is amazed that I would ever have a live-aboard home after this experience; she asks how I ended up aboard the *Lui-Nu*. I tell her that when I returned from points south of the border the year before and found out that the man to whom I had sold my transportation shuttle company in Denver had not been making the payments to me or to the vehicle leasing company, I was forced to file for bankruptcy, which eventually led to my departure from Vail. I traveled west in search of a prospering location to find a job, perhaps in the restaurant business, and instead found that I was no longer in demand in the work force.

I decided to contact a woman I met in St John, USVI, while attending a wedding for my old friend, David Luchetti. She had a home rental company on the Island and had helped with planning their wedding. She let me know that if I ever wanted to move to St. John, she could help me with a place to stay. When I called, she said the offer was still on the table and that I could stay with her and her boyfriend until I got settled. I made the move to St. John and, for three years, worked with home rental companies doing maintenance and re-models.

I was content for the time being and was settling into life on the Island, but wanted to find some permanent housing which was very expensive in this little piece of paradise. I decided to buy a Hurricane Hugo boat that had been sitting in the mangroves for almost two years, rotting away.

I called her the *Lui-Nu* because she was the start of my new life. I spent the next fourteen months rebuilding the boat and, of course, lived on it during the process. Life on the *Lui-Nu* turned into a great adventure and when I was ready to leave, I sold it for a formidable price. This hard-earned cash helped me return to Vail and eventually embark on this bike adventure. . .

Jackie reminds me that St. John, USVI, is where she and her husband, Rich, first lived together before getting married and moving to the Seattle area. We smile and agree that it is indeed a small world.

Saturday morning at the Wood house does not begin with cartoons on the tube like in many American homes, but the whole family dresses and heads out to see Rich play soccer. I take the opportunity to stay home and catch up on my writing. Tomorrow we are planning to take the apples we picked from their orchard and loaded in bushel baskets to the old-fashion general store in town to make our own cider because it is Apple Press Day on the Island.

I call up my old friend and roommate, Dave Dasse, who now lives in Canon Beach, Oregon and make a new plan. He and his wife will be camping next week just fifty miles, as the crow flies, from here and he invites me to join them for some gourmet camping and a priceless opportunity to renew our friendship.

I immediately feel an inner urge to get moving again and agree to meet them at Graves Creek Campground on Tuesday. I am feeling the draw of the road pulling me away from the more traditional life-style Jackie and Rich have invited me to share. I take out my maps from my panniers and calculate that the ride by bike will be 200 miles. I will leave on Monday, and head out on Highway #101E going south and ride to #101W before turning north toward Quinault Lake in the Olympic National Forest where I will meet Dave and Bonnie.

That night Rich, Jackie and I have our last dinner out on Bainbridge Island at another old house that has been converted into a restaurant. The three of us convince ourselves that we want to find some type of entertainment but, as they had suspected and tried to warn me, nothing like that is available on the Island so we find ourselves back at the house by 10 p.m.

I am grateful for their generosity and hospitality and want to pay them back by offering to paint the 100 yards of fence out back the next day; and if I am lucky, carve out a little time to watch Sunday NFL football.

We say our good-bys on Monday morning as the family leaves to begin another week filled with work, sports and everyday tasks that end each day with conversation around the dinner table where accomplishments and struggles are recognized and supported. I wonder if I will ever have that again in my life. I had many rich conversations at dinner with Moe and Ailish when I was living with them in Vail and feel a tug on my heartstrings as I drift off to sleep.

RIDING TO
THE RAIN FOREST

thirteen

I notice the date, October 10th, on the calendar in the Woods' kitchen and know my time may be running out on the Indian summer I have been enjoying. I begin to pack my panniers and by 9 a.m. I am once again in the saddle of my Jamison Coda. That change of weather, the old gentleman I met a few days ago mentioned, seems to have arrived. The skies are overcast, with hints of gray clouds filling in the horizon. I bundle up and prepare myself for a cool day of riding with the threat of being sprayed with some rain drops. Yes, my first big rainy day on the road presents itself for the next four hours and thirty-five miles. Riding in the rain is quite different because you aren't able to focus on the scenery around you; instead, you are forced to concentrate on the road ahead and your side mirror. I am finding this new experience uninteresting and feel as if I am removed from the scene. My solar-powered computer quits working almost immediately. When intermittent periods of sun return, I change my clothes. Riding along the road, my front pack is now serving as a clothes-line and must be an amusing sight to see a bike rider drying his clothes in the wind as he pedals along.

I can't help but chuckle as I think back to 1968 and recall a story about another time when I had laundry hanging out to dry inappropriately. Colorado's governor, John Love, had been invited to Vail by the mayor. The talk of the town was to put our best foot forward to impress the governor. A few of us wanted to show him our version of a European hotel. My old friend, Lee Caracelli, had a sign business at the time. She made a sign in the European style saying *Polish Pension,* and displayed it on the side of the building between the Rucksack and the Red Lion. We proceeded to string up a clothesline and hang long johns and some lingerie on the line. We were fully aware that the dignitaries would be walking up and down Bridge Street on their tour of the town and could not help but catch a glimpse of the sign. Needless to say, we did not make the front page of the Vail Trail. In fact, our prank was discovered before the tour began and we were told to take it down quickly. Our little incident may have eventually led to Vail's strict sign ordinance; for us it was just another way to create entertainment for ourselves.

I ride down Highway #101 to a road that cuts across to Highway #12 then down to a town called Montesano where there is one motel with a no vacancy sign posted out front and a state park campground. There are no signs as to how far Sylvia Campground is, but I forge ahead in the softly falling rain while darkness closes in. Luckily, the distance to the site is only one and a half miles. I reach the entrance none too soon as I am becoming chilled to the bone. It is after 9 p.m. when I get my tent set up and crawl into my sleeping bag, which feels cold and clammy making warming up in it difficult. I get out of my tent and layer-up. When I crawl back into my sleeping bag I am dressed in my riding clothes, jacket and socks and remain that way until 3 a.m. when I am finally able to take my socks and jacket off. I drift off to sleep after making a review in my mind of today's 110-mile ride. When I finally awake the next morning and poke my head out of the tent, I see that I am sleeping under tall fir trees with a carpet of pine needles surrounding the platform where I pitched my tent in the dark.

Today the skies are a soft gray and the temperature is a cold, damp thirty degrees. I glance toward the misty horizon and take in the view. The campground is in a low valley surrounded by mountains so I conclude that, if the sun comes out today, it won't shower my tent with warmth until 10 a.m. or so. I decide to brave the cold and layer-up before breaking camp. I am on the road at 8 a.m. and stop two miles later to have coffee, warm up and do some writing. The sky is beginning to break up at 8:45 a.m. and I am optimistic that the day will evolve into a beautiful one. My mind keeps coming back to the fact that my bike chain fell off first thing today and several times yesterday. I wonder why this is starting to happen now, but can't seem to make sense of it at the moment.

I take my mind off of the bike problem and float back to the '70s in Vail when Dave Dasse and I became friends. More than thirty years ago, Dave had one of the original rafting companies called Der Raftmeister. In winter, the shop was transformed into Der Skimeister. Dave and I lived together in a third-floor, two-bedroom apartment at Breakaway West, with a balcony-view of one of the few swimming pools in Vail, Colorado. I was in the bar business at the time and arrived home no earlier than two in the morning, while David was out of the door before 6 a.m. so our paths rarely crossed. I realize that it's never too late to get to know someone better.

This seems like as good a time as any to commence my ride as I am as warm as I will get on this chilly Pacific Northwest October morning. The cold, damp weather is creating havoc with my body and I have to wrap my knee after forty-five miles on the road. Besides the dreary weather and achy knee, I am shocked by the austerity of the surroundings caused by clear cutting, and find that riding without a scenic view is very monotonous. One after another timber trucks pass. Luckily, I have plenty of room on the wide shoulder. I have mixed emotions when I see the new tree growth along the road and know these saplings will not reach maturity for seventy-five or eighty years, but, at least, the trees have been replaced. The new scars are ugly and it appears that timbering is taking place in the National Parks as well.

I turn into the Quinault Lake Road and realize I have entered the Olympic National Forest. Within two miles, I reach the seventy-year-old lodge that is advertising rooms from $60 to $80 a night. The ancient structure, built of timbers and covered on the outside with cedar shake shingles, is not glamorous or even particularly majestic like some of the other National Park lodges I have seen on this trip. It sits on the lake and has a row of long wooden benches and a few Adirondack chairs on a large deck, positioned for the best views of the water. The lodge inside has a pleasant ambiance with a warm fire blazing in the restaurant fireplace. Just beyond the restaurant is a bar and game room with a few people casually wrapped up in conversation with one another. I set my jacket down and glance out the window at the unfamiliar view of the large green lawn in front of the lodge, facing the lake. I have some time to wait until Dave and Bonnie arrive so I check out the prices on food at the store across the street and notice they are more than reasonable for an isolated park.

The Rain Forest Resort is just down the road one mile, so I pedal over to check it out and find the world's largest Spruce tree, which is 1,000 years old and measures fifty-two feet across and ninety-six feet around. This wonder of nature is climbing skyward 191 feet and is dwarfing some really large Hemlock, Douglas firs and Western Red Cedar trees. Pristine, glacier-fed waters lap at the beach in front of the Rain Forest Resort. It also has a small restaurant and bar with $4.44 spaghetti dinner night tonight and a general store, hotel, and campground. I'm supposed to meet Dave at the other Lodge at 4:30 p.m. so I head back up the road to change clothes and clean up in the hotel bathroom.

The foliage in the Quinault Rain Forest is thick and green and the animals are making noises, just out of my sight. I am delighted to be in a temperate rain forest for the first time in my life and have actually envisioned it this way. As I glance up again at the towering trees, I can see why this is known as the Valley of the Giants. The Olympic National Forest has five major landscape settings beside the temperate rain forest. There are also rugged mountains, large lowland lakes, cascading rivers and salt water beaches, home to some amazing flora and fauna just waiting to be explored.

Lake Quinault, surrounded by mossy, old-growth trees, is about the size of the large Dillon Reservoir near Vail, Colorado. I look at the lake in the distance and see only one powerboat and not a single sailboat. Then I remember that the busy summer tourist season has ended. The resorts stay open year round although the campgrounds will be closing soon. Along the park roads, there are private homes that seem to be inhabited mostly by long-hair hippie folks.

Dave and Bonnie arrive at the Lodge for cocktails and we catch up on what's been happening since we saw each other in Vail about ten years ago. We know that we will have plenty of time to share more stories in the next few days so we load my bike into their pick-up truck and drive down to Graves Creek Campground, about fifteen miles away, for one of the most delicious dinners of my entire bike trip. My friends serve freshly picked chanterelle mushrooms, shrimp salad and wine to go with the potatoes and steak that we grill over the campfire under a star-studded sky. I am actually thinking that I should bring cooking gear on my next trip!

I feel intimately connected to nature when I am camping and will miss this when the journey has ended. I fall asleep in my tent listening to the sounds of the forest and wonder if a bobcat or black bear is watching the fading embers of our campfire and hoping to find a morsel of food to fill his hungry belly. I lay my hand on my tiny container of bear spray, and I forcefully refocus my thoughts on the fact that, including the seventy miles I rode today, I have covered a total of 1,840 miles.

The warm weather and brilliant blue sky inspire us to spend another day in the Olympic National Park. We hike into the rain forest, scattered with large moss-covered trees on a well-maintained trail, picking a pound or two of chanterelle mushrooms along the way. We pass only four other hikers and spot a group of female elk, led by one imposing male with a proud eight-point rack.

The colors in the afternoon sky are settling as we hike back to camp and prepare a huge dinner with more mushrooms than we can eat. The moon is about half full and is very bright this evening as it rises over our camp. The night seems quite warm compared to the previous ones. I find that having a drop cloth under my tent makes a big difference in the warmth and dryness. Tonight, I even heat a rock and wrap it in a towel to lie next to my head. This works very well, and the rock actually stays warm until 3 a.m.

On Thursday morning, it is a warm fifty degrees with clouds indicating that rain might be in the forecast. We decide to pack up after breakfast and go for another walk around the old lodge so that Dave and Bonnie can see the gardens and architecture by daylight. I notice that the rain gauge at the lodge goes up to seventeen feet, but the yearly mark, so far, is only at seven feet. I recall that when I rode through this area yesterday, I could see the ugly evidence of the drought everywhere. Dave, on the other hand, feels lucky that his vacation over the last six days here in the Olympic National Forest has not included a single drop of rain.

We pull out of the park campground at 12:30 p.m. with a full load in the pick-up truck. Dave and Bonnie do not travel light, but have generously added my bike and gear to the truck bed, just as the first drops of rain fall from the gray October sky. This early autumn rainfall continues for the next 165 miles until we reach Cannon Beach. We pass a dozen bikers along the way including one couple with a flat tire, who seem to have the task of changing the tire just about wrapped up. As we cross the half-mile-long Astoria Bridge, which goes over the Columbia River, the winds pick up as well. Glancing out of the truck window, I see that the road down to the river only has a two-to three-foot shoulder for bikers, but as we near Cannon Beach the bike lane gets wider and is now marked as a bike path leading the rest of the way through Oregon. This idea of pedaling along on a scenic bike path without being bothered by traffic intrigues me, but my interest in riding at the moment is dampened by the fact that raindrops are still pounding on the windshield and the winds are gusting to thirty miles per hour.

My first impression of Cannon Beach is that of a cute tourist town with a nice charm to it. It covers about three blocks between Highway #101 and the Pacific Ocean along the Northern Oregon coast. I can see why it has become a popular vacation resort. The town extends for four miles along the Pacific and reminds me more of a village as it is adorned with many gorgeous flowerpots, interspersed with lots of places to relax and enjoy the view. It looks like the premier sculpture in Cannon Beach, Haystack Rock, was carved by Mother Nature and sticks its head out of the Ocean just off shore. There are many shops nestled in one-story wooden buildings lining the streets.

We stop first at Bonnie's bookbinding shop. She makes fabric-covered journals which are sold and shipped all over the country. Next stop is Dave's 2,000 square foot T-shirt store in downtown Cannon Beach on a prominent corner location. He introduces me to his partner who runs their small jewelry store next door.

We pile back into the truck and proceed to the home that they built at the top of a hill overlooking the ocean. It is a beautiful modern house with a unique design, warm feeling and an incredible view.

Bonnie motions for me to come over near the sound system to listen to a demo tape she made when she had her own female punk-rock band in 1988. She played guitar, lead vocal and wrote most of the songs the group performed. She sounded very professional with a groovy voice and a loud back-up band which made me a bit surprised that she didn't continue in the music business. She wanted me to know that she gave up this dream for Dave and the tone in her voice tells me she sometimes has regrets. As the night closes in, the wind and rain continue and we all feel lucky to be in a cozy, warm home. I fade out of our conversations from time to time and focus on the thought in my head of how I once again lucked out along this journey and was able to move south 165 miles in the dryness of a moving vehicle. I remember one of Lance Armstrong's pearls of wisdom, "Don't ride in the rain," and I am comforted that I am not a *Prima Dona*, but just following the words of a wiser and more experienced biker.

All week long there are periods of drizzle as I explore more than ninety-three miles along the coast with the use of Dave's truck or by bike when the weather co-operates. I observe one little tourist town after another as I meander down Highway #101. I am aware, as the weekend approaches, that hoards of visitors will descend on these towns to replenish the coffers in the many shops and restaurants that depend on the tourist industry to sustain their economy.

I travel as far south as Tillamook and the scenery is awesome. I take the bike down a winding, twisting road in Ecola Creek State Park which is enclosed in deep, dark rain forest foliage and I follow the signs to Indian Beach. The views of the shoreline from the parking lot alone will stir your soul. I take the Tillamook Head Lighthouse trail, which wanders some six miles to a seaside picnic viewpoint above the crescent beach. This is a good point to see Goonies Rock which has an unmistakable giant hole in the middle of the slab that is firmly anchored in the sea.

As the tide goes out, I take a walk to look for pool surprises hidden among the smooth pebbles that make up part of the shoreline. There is even an amazing little stream that is running through the cobblestone beach and some picturesque grottos carved by the sea into the rocky cliffs. I would like to be here to see the whales breeching off shore, but have arrived a little late in the year for that spectacle.

The imposing facade of Tillamook Lighthouse sits in the Pacific Ocean one mile away and remains a mystery because it is the only Oregon lighthouse that cannot be accessed by walking to it. I have read stories about the terrifying construction of this project, which was completed in 1881. I imagine the waves slamming into the rock and horrifying winds howling as a team of workers try to set a post into concrete. When it was completed, a team of four men at a time manned the lighthouse and were stuck there for a month before relief came. Food and supplies were delivered by ships, and a giant winch was used to bring the materials ashore. It was finally decommissioned in 1957 and all that remains are the stories that were written about the storms endured on the rock and a crumbling structure left to the mercy of Mother Nature.

It occurs to me that the days are getting shorter and I should return to the parking lot before a late afternoon rain douses me and darkens the sky before its time. I return to Bonnie and Dave's house just in time to observe one of Cannon Beach's famous sunsets and later join Dave's partner, Jim, and his wife, Carolyn, for a dinner in town.

Sunday arrives and, before I know it, the day has started to fade at the same time the exodus of tourists from this little coastal paradise, once again return it to the locals who have chosen to enjoy life between the up and down flow of the crowds. I offer to cook my last dinner with Bonnie and Dave. Of course salmon and homemade pesto pasta with Caesar salad are on the menu. Rain raps against the living room windows as we chuckle about growing up in Vail and that leaving was the only thing that could have saved us both from being drowned in the rivers of alcohol and drugs that flowed once-upon-a-time through this classy resort town.

Dave and Bonnie are fantastic hosts and have really taken good care of me. Dave is going on a buying trip to Seattle on Monday morning and, since it rained all evening and well into the night and is still dripping this morning, I happily accept a ride to Portland with him. He deposits me and my bike at the train station at 8:30 a.m. where we say good-bye. We both smile as he extends his hand along with an invitation to return anytime. Just inside the station, I break down my bike and check it in before walking downtown under a cool drizzle. I hop on the old-fashioned streetcar for a cruise through downtown Portland and, thirty miles later, reach the end of the line ($1.30 round trip).

They have a great transportation system in Portland. In fact, I discover that Portland is known for its strong investment in a light rail system supported by a Metro. I then discover that Portland, the City of Roses, is also famous for its large number of microbreweries. I don't have enough time to investigate this specialty of the third most populated city in the Pacific Northwest, but can't help but notice that it is clean, quiet and emits little pollutants. Paddleboats cruise the river and the convention center towers give the skyline an interesting look. The colors are changing along the river and in the parks. The oak and maple leaves are a brilliant orange, red and purple. I take a stroll through old town before heading back to the train station.

I board my southbound train and we finally leave at 2:25 p.m. only ten minutes late. As I glance off at Mt. St. Helens in the distance, I feel a bit of excitement about being on the move again, and am looking forward to the countryside, sunshine and warmer weather I hope to encounter as I travel south along the Pacific coastline.

fourteen

I board the train south, find my seat and settle in for this part of my journey. I glance out the window at the soft blue sky with an assortment of billowy clouds whizzing by which confirms that I am not traveling at bike speed. The day passes with the blur of the scenery outside the window, reminding me of my life in the 1980s when I used to take the train to Lake Tahoe to visit friends. I met a lot of interesting people on those trips maybe because I was younger and frequented the bar car. I recall that sometimes I even booked a sleeper suite; that would have been a great idea for this night.

As dinnertime approaches, I meander to the club car where I meet a few interesting people who are traveling to California. We spend time talking and have a bite to eat together. After dinner, we go our separate ways and I am resigned to an early bedtime. I am lucky enough to have two empty seats together and the temperature is warm and comfortable. I glance out and notice that the drizzle that has been off and on all afternoon has stopped and the moon is peeping over the trees, lighting up the night. It looks plump and round, but I know the moon won't be full for a few more days.

The full moon became a very important element in the travel that Moe and I did over the years. It began with her trip to the Virgin Islands when her flight home was canceled because of foul weather. We walked back from the airport to the ferry in a drizzle, and went across the sea to St. John where the *Lui-Nu* (my home on the water) was moored. Like this evening, the skies had cleared and we spent the night under a full moon. As our friendship grew, we escaped to many far-away places and each time tried to plan the trip around the cycle of the full moon. I start to wonder just how many more full moons we will be apart. Will she be ready for me to return to Vail and build a life together? And am I ready for this step? I notice I am giving it more thought now that I am on the last leg of my bicycle journey. Sleeping on a train seat is not that comfortable, but I manage a few hours. At 6:30 a.m. I wake up and go into the dining car for coffee and cereal. I am supposed to arrive at 7:40 a.m., but we are running thirty minutes behind.

As we enter the San Francisco area, the sun rises with a backdrop of a brilliant blue sky and the warmth I had hoped for. I step off the train, locate my bike and think, confidence is everything! I assemble the bike outside the station and am on the road by 9:30 a.m., only to realize that I have no idea how I am going to get over the Golden Gate Bridge.

I pedal onto the expressway and am stopped almost immediately by a highway crew person who is as friendly and supportive as he is large. He points out a rule that forbids bikes on the freeway and on the Golden Gate Bridge; he kindly tells me about the Oakland Passenger Ferry.

I immediately head to the nearest marina, two miles away, to inquire about its whereabouts. A soft-spoken woman gives me some lengthy directions to a spot about eight miles away. I quickly realize that this is going to be another process of trial and error. I stop to get redirected and am given the suggestion to use the BART train. This makes the most sense to me; the BART train is closer, cheaper, has more departures and can take me further. I find the station a few miles away; and without dawdling, I fill out a form to bring the bike along for only $1.85. I board the train with my bike just as it is departing.

I take the BART train from Oakland that goes under the bay through San Francisco then out to Daley City, about twenty-five miles away, where I get off the train and pedal towards Highway #35 to the Coast Highway #1. I am feeling a certain freedom as I barrel down the highway with flashbacks about riding Independence Pass outside of Aspen. The only difference is the scenery. The crashing Pacific is now on my right and in Aspen I would be glancing down at the winding river as I pedaled the switchbacks to the foot of the steep canyon and back up again. Maybe it is because I am not paying attention to the present or perhaps the vibration of the bicycle alerts me that a problem is developing. I am going down hill when I am drawn back to the now and hear a screeching noise. I am shocked as my bike has never done anything this erratic before. I immediately realize that a spoke has snapped and the rear wheel has gone out of round. I am forced to spend the next twenty miles riding slowly while looking for a bike shop. At 3 p.m., I finally find one at Half Moon Bay and the energetic mechanics are able to start working on it right away. Lunch is long overdue and I am grateful to be in a spot where restaurants are open. One hour and $30 later, I am back in business.

The sun is still strong and the air is warm, but I am struck by the realization that I have only traveled forty-three miles so far. I need to be thinking about where I will spend the night. Other than the restrictions placed on me by Mother Nature, I am free from the tyranny of a timetable. My map shows that I have two choices for the night: a hostel at Pigeon Point about thirty miles down the road or a campground a little farther along. I find this section of the road very easy to ride. The terrain offers me long up-hill stretches, followed by speedy descents mixed with a fair amount of flat riding. The cliffs are very close to the shoulder and, because of wind gusts, I have to use my brake quite often on the downhill.

My knee starts to really ache, so I employ three aspirins and the knee wrap to tame the pain. I am relieved to see the sign for the Pigeon Point Hostel which turns out to be the old lighthouse property. I'm not sure what I expect to see, but the prospects intrigue me. The three separate lighthouse keeper's quarters have been converted into dorm rooms. I don't hesitate to pay the $13 fee for a bed without linens for the night. If I had been a member of a Youth Hostel Organization, I would only have to hand over $10. I lean against the desk and read the rules of the hostel and notice that everyone is required to sign up for a morning chore. Taking out the trash was my task of choice.

The hostel provides clean bunk beds in each of the rooms; one male; the other, female. There is a community shower and toilet as well as a kitchen and living room. Eight travelers have checked in already, mostly women, and they are all in the kitchen cooking. I tell them that I will trade some of my trail mix for steak, but no takers!

This seems like a great opportunity to catch up on my journal entries. Because there is no light in the bedrooms, I settle at a table and chair in the living room. There is no TV or radio so the laughter of the ladies is all there is for background noise at the moment.

I stroll outside and find a rock on the point from which to watch the sun go down behind the 115-foot lighthouse which is located on a bluff above the Pacific Ocean. This is one of the tallest lighthouses in America. Opened in 1872, it once guided mariners traveling between Santa Cruz and Half Moon Bay. I chat with a mental health nurse from San Francisco who is also taking in the view. We spot porpoises 100 feet off shore; she is delighted to have this first-hand experience. She tells me that from December through March, this stretch of the ocean is the breeding grounds for the gigantic elephant seals. This also becomes a great lookout point for whale watching from January to September. Unfortunately, this is off-season for all but the porpoises. She described how, earlier this morning, she had ventured down to the tidal pools, located just beyond the hostel grounds, and found them rich in plant and animal life.

We watch the mesmerizing waves pound the shore and an almost-full moon rise from inland behind the lighthouse; making a great photo op. We are both disappointed that the hot tub, located on the point, is closed as the building in which it is partially housed is being painted. I begin to tell her about how and where my bike journey began as my memory brings me back to Steamboat Inn B & B and how Moe and I enjoyed the hot tub there on several occasions.

My knee is screaming, and I am glad that I did not choose to pedal the few more miles down the road and stay at the campground. The opportunity to socialize with other travelers is much more stimulating. I glance over my shoulder as I am walking back to the bunk house and I see a field of pumpkins growing on the fertile marine terrace near the point. I realize that it is fall and winter is not far behind in the high country in Colorado. I wonder if my footsteps will take me back to Moe and a new life in Colorado.

The next morning, after completing my chores, I say good-bye to the lady travelers, noting some of their suggestions for future stops, and I am on my way. The temperature today varies, as well as the fog. Finally, at 2:30 p.m., the skies clear completely and temperatures warm up.

I try to locate John Purcell, the past owner of Purcell's Restaurant, a landmark in the Lionshead section of Vail. He is the next person on my list of past acquaintances to search out along my journey. He is not listed in information and the telephone numbers I have do not connect me with him; but I am not giving up yet. The breeze is full-on this afternoon. The fog that enshrouds the bay has retreated from the coast, offering a stunning view as I make a plan to end my ride today over-looking the Pacific Ocean.

The scenery is spectacular as I pedal easily, with no hint of knee pain, along the California coast. The most beautiful vistas come to view when riding the Monterey Peninsula through the manicured stretches of Pebble Beach and Spy Glass Golf Clubs, contrasted with the rough jagged coast with seals and deer around every corner. The animals are so tame that a golfer in a cart stops to hit his shot while twenty or more deer lie around him without flinching. I spot the Pacific Grove Public

Course on the ocean, which only costs $15 for a round of golf, versus the $250 fees or more at Pebble Beach. Since I am no longer a golfer, I pedal easily past both of the attractions.

The map shows that the ride from Monterey to Carmel on Highway #1 is only four or five miles. I decide to take the seventeen-mile detour on Crespi Lane into Carmel. I am happy I do because of the scenery. I have been leaving messages at Mission Hills for John Purcell all day, but unfortunately he has not been able to receive my calls. Up ahead I spot Carmel, located on a gentle rising headland above a sculpted rocky shore. It is well known for its ridiculously inflated real estate prices, neat rows of quaint shops and storybook English cottages along Ocean Avenue. It has a thick air of pretension; it is peppered with art galleries and mock-Tudor tearooms. Other than the Carmel Mission Basilica and a couple of small museums, there is little to intrigues me, except the fact that there are graves of 3,000 Native Americans laid to rest in the cemetery. I would like to find out more about this interesting fact, but since I am not traveling with a laptop and no Internet shops have opened along my route, I will wait.

Carmel-by-the-Sea is a perfect destination for a girlfriend's weekend, but I have no interest in lingering in this paradise of the rich and famous. I will not list this in my book of places to revisit other than what Mother Nature has created. It is now 5 p.m. and I give up the search for my friend and ride out of Carmel hoping to find a cheap motel or campground.

Unfortunately, there are none. About twenty miles later I decide to camp along the edge of a cliff, situated thirty feet from the highway. It is probably illegal, but my options are limited as dusk is already setting in and Big Sur is forty-five minutes further along this shoulder-less stretch of Highway #1. I finish my four ounces of trail mix and the last of my water. I will sleep wrapped in my new eight-by-ten-foot tarp and sandwich my sleeping bag and pad inside it. I don't want the tent up in case a cop drives by and spots it. There is no sign of rain. I imagine the fog will be getting thicker, but I decide I will risk it. It turns out that I don't have to be afraid of the darkness as the moon has come up and fishing boats, with glaring lights to attract fish, are working off the point where I am camped.

I lie awake and wonder if nightfall will ever arrive. I begin to reflect on the day and my ride down the coast around Monterey, California.

Before I arrived in Monterey, I pedaled through a few small towns on the Peninsula, including Santa Cruz, which seemed like a fun town to visit. They had an amusement park located on the boardwalk, adjacent to the beach. A lot of Victorian homes also backed up to the sand and sea. Bike paths are abundant in this part of California and I was excited to be able to ride for miles without having to think about car and truck traffic. When there was no bike path, there were excellent bike lanes on the highways and coastal roads.

I recalled how I was overcome by a horrible smell that reminded me of dead animals, but later found out that it was the after-harvest smell of Brussels sprouts. On the flip side of riding in this agricultural area, was the presence of numerous fresh fruit and vegetable stands, set up along the roadside. My body was craving the sweet, juicy options for my afternoon snack so I purchased a few peaches and plums for dinner.

Back at my campsite, with the marine-blue waves crashing below, the tarp is working well to keep me warm and dry. I finally fall asleep to the sound of seals barking in the background until something black, about two inches high and wide, crawls nearby. When I move to turn on my light, it quickly runs off into the low-lying shrubs. I never did see what it is. My imagination takes over as I visualize a huge tarantula invading my sleeping space over and over during the night. Dawn breaks upon the horizon and whatever it was never did attack me.

To my delight, a warm fifty-five-degree sunny day presents itself as I open my eyes and immediately put the memories of the creepy black creature out of my mind. I am puzzled that my sleeping bag is wet on the outside, even though it was covered with a tarp, and my head is bone dry. I put the sleeping-bag mystery aside, as instinct tells me that I need to vacate my illegal, road-side camping site and move along, even though it is only 8 a.m.

I misjudge the temperature and dress in way too many layers before packing up and heading down the road looking for Big Sur. Within fifteen minutes, I strip down to shorts and a long sleeve shirt. I notice on the map that the Big Sur Region covers the road on Highway #1 from Carmel to San Simeon south. The road ahead is steep, with two bridges spanning gorges next to the ocean you often see in car advertisements. With every long, uphill section, there is the ride down; jacket on, jacket off for each encounter. The scenery is spectacular and I see very expensive, propane-operated homes, hidden in the windswept trees and craggy cliffs. The shrubs on the hillsides are not large and look like big artichokes shaded in color from yellow to purple. The drive takes almost two hours and the signs suggest ten miles per hour for cars. Bikes are able to handle curves much better so I stop long enough to replenish my body with the remaining half of a power bar and pick up the pace on this downhill ride. When I arrive at a restaurant in Big Sur, I have an appetite and thirst equally big. I spread my sleeping bag over my bike to dry and go in for a huge breakfast in a very friendly establishment, The River Inn, with a motel by the same name next door.

The friendly waitress tells me that it is almost Monarch butterfly season and asks if I have seen any on my ride. They should be migrating south in masses to the same winter roosts, often the exact same Eucalyptus trees, in the central part of Mexico where they were born last year. They only make this two-way trip once in their lifetime. It is really their children's grandchildren who return south the following fall. I report that I have not seen a single of these winged beauties, but perhaps I will be lucky enough to ride along with them on their journey south.

The dot on the map, known as Big Sur, is actually inland off the coast and consists of little more than a couple of campgrounds. I head out and up to a summit five miles away. With only two miles to go to the top, I pop another spoke and the wheel goes out of round. By the time I get to the summit, the wheel is in very bad shape and I pull over to loosen the rear brake pads. I try to hitch a ride for almost thirty minutes, but don't have any luck. There is little traffic and no trucks have come by. I am forced to start riding slowly with a lot of brake action.

The town of Lucia is twenty miles ahead. Eight miles into the ride to Lucia, I spot a tow truck jumping a car battery. I convince the truck driver to give me a ride into town. He is not very friendly and wants $5 for the lift. I gladly pay it, but to my surprise the town of Lucia only consists of a restaurant, gas station and general store. Luck is on my side when I meet three bikers from San Francisco who offer me an extra spoke from their repair kit. Since I have never changed a spoke before, they help me with the task and true the wheel as well. At 2 p.m., I am back in business. The friendly bicycle riders are also headed in the same direction, except they have no gear to haul.

I tell them I will meet them tonight in Cambria, fifty miles away. I settle in for another ride with spectacular views of the cliffs rising 1,000 feet over the ocean with its rushing tide. The road hugs the rocky hillside and goes back down, then up, as it spans four or five more bridges with a view that fills me with awe. Homes are tucked away in spots you can't believe. The Ocean in this area is clear and blue, something I did not equate with the Pacific coast. There is nothing between Big Sur and San Luis Obispo, 135 miles away, only a few one-store towns.

Cambria, a larger town at the foot of the Hearst Castle, seems to only exist for the castle. In 1927, William Randolph Hearst told architect Julia Morgan that he wanted to build a little something on his piece of land in California. Eighteen years later the Moorish-design castle with 165 rooms on 127 acres was completed. I am disappointed that the Hearst Castle is closed when I pedal by. I would love to have been able to tour the rooms, terraces, and especially the pools and gardens. I see motels advertised for $40 and a restaurant row that spans the next 200 yards and then spreads out on both sides of the highway. I observe all I can while driving through the town and then drive out one mile to a nice campground crowded with friendly bikers. To my delight, the campground offers hot showers. I chat it up with the other bikers and get some tips for the journey ahead.

The cyclists who had helped me earlier in the day with my broken spoke were spending their nights in hotels, not campgrounds so I did not see them at the camp. I had eaten a pocket pizza for dinner at the deli in Cambria, so my night ends up being an early one. I make a few notes in my journal about the 100 miles of road I covered today. I wonder what all the broken windshield glass on the coast road was from. I feel lucky that I have had another day of safe traveling while seeing some of the most amazing scenery this country has to offer. Before falling asleep, I make a wish on a falling star for more of the same tomorrow.

I am amazed that it is already forty-eight degrees at 8 a.m. The heat from the early morning sun is drying my tent, so I have some time to explore the area before taking off along the coast on what appears to be another beautiful day. I am excited to be wearing shorts and a short sleeve shirt by 9 a.m.

I head up to Cambria Village, not to be confused with Cambria Grove through which I came last night, about four miles down the road. This charming little village is partly on the ocean with shops and restaurants across from the highway. There are no bike shops in the area so I am not going to be able to pick up any extra spokes.

By 10 a.m. I am on the road again and headed along Highway #1 inland for twenty miles and then back to the water at a town that has 20,000 people but no bike shops. Farther down the road, where the famous Morro Rock is located, I find the larger town of Morro with 30,000 inhabitants, and still no bicycle shop. I cruise the waterfront and end up at a dead end, but am glad I took the time to explore. Morro Rock is actually a large dormant volcano located a few hundred feet off the shore of Morro Bay, California. This 576-foot spectacle stands at the harbor and is connected by a causeway to the shore. Only the base can be visited; climbing the rock is positively off-limits. This landmark has been important to sailors and travelers for hundreds of years but even more important to the Chumask Indian tribe. In prehistoric times, the tribe had a settlement near the twenty-million-year-old rock. It has always been a sacred site to tribe members who are allowed to climb the rock for their annual solstice ceremony. The rock is also a peregrine falcon reserve, but there did not seem to be any soaring around this morning.

On my way out of town, I stop to enjoy my first TCBY yogurt of the day. Before long, my tracks are again leading up to Highway #1, which turns into an expressway when I get just past Morro. About that time, my San Francisco bicycle-friends finally catch up and, as they pass by, we give each other the high-five. I imagine that I have surprised them by being ahead of them while carrying a full load of gear in my panniers.

I continue another twelve miles to San Luis Obispo and, from my perspective, find the highway very noisy. An Asian rider pulls up next to me on his bike and gives me directions to a bike shop in San Luis Obispo, just off the highway. I pull into a bicycle shop where they give me some free drink mix and a spoke and don't charge any tax on the $8 spoke wrench I have purchased. They share some directions that lead me out of town and away from traffic. My tracks are taking me in the direction of Pismo Beach.

Because a bridge is out, I am forced to take an alternative route and follow the detour signs. Highway #1 becomes #101, and, surprise, no bikes are allowed. I head inland and work my way back to the ocean.

Besides the spectacular view of the crashing waves, I have a bike lane again and a lot less traffic. I ride around Pismo Beach and get directions from a friendly traffic cop to Pismo State Park, about eight miles down the road. I actually drive past it; because it is only 3 p.m. and my odometer says I have only traveled seventy-five miles today. About a half mile past the park sign, I stop on the side of the road to look at the map and see that I'm going inland again. I turn around and notice that the breeze from the Pacific Ocean is blowing in my face, and it takes a little work to make it back to a pleasant, clean campground. This little treasure of a *hotel under the stars* is 200 yards from the beach and the $3-a-night fee includes showers. It is such a nice day, I decide to stop riding and enjoy the beach.

I find my tent is still wet from last night, and I am glad that I have the time to set it up early to let the warm ocean breezes dry the moisture. I meet my neighbor, who just came down from Alaska on a bike. We chat a bit, but I am more interested in taking a hot shower. The next important thing on my agenda is to find a laundromat and do something about the mounting pile of dirty clothes. I head one and a half miles into the nearby town of Oceana and do my laundry. I'm feeling like a million bucks now. I have some greasy Mexican food at a stand by the laundromat before going back to watch the sunset.

Toward evening I glance out at the sky. It is hard to tell where the ocean ends and the clouds, now purpling as the sun sets, begin. I decide it is time to try to call Gilby and Karen, more characters from the Vail restaurant scene, who now live in Santa Barbara. Luck would have it that they are out of town, so I decide to stay another day here in this little Pacific Coast paradise.

The beach is 150 yards deep. Cars, campers, ATV's and even horses are allowed on the beach. The beach area is patrolled well and remains very clean. The campground is located just off the beach. I can walk 150 feet over a sand dune to my tent. Weekend campers have already started arriving and setting up their gear all around me. I know that I am better off remaining where I am for the weekend as the Saturday and Sunday traffic will most likely be pretty heavy on the highway. If I travel on Sunday it will be only as far as Santa Barbara. My map shows that the road south from Santa Barbara narrows, so I go to sleep tonight absolutely convinced that my plan to depart on Monday is logical. The sound of the surf plays a word game in my mind as I try to fall asleep: sun, sky, surf, sand, sails, shore, smooth, surge, suck, spray, sweep…

Unfortunately, this tranquil paradise turns into a chaotic scene during the night, with a brawl in one area and a big party, accompanied by a lot of noise, in the other. This turn of events has left me with an uncertain feeling that seems to have unraveled the perfect plan I formulated last night.

The campground is finally quiet at 9 a.m. I can once again hear the lapping waves on the shore as I pack up my tent and pedal across the street to a diner for a cup of coffee and a piece of pie. The sky is a soft gray and the temperatures are already warm. I am thinking that the cloud cover will be good since I am going inland through dry, barren countryside for the early part of the day. I am surrounded by patches of land where zucchinis and berries are coming in while a new crop has started growing under plastic sheeting, and yet another field is being tilled for the next planting. The color contrasts are interesting to look at, but it is far from the dappled green of the forests with pale green ferns that I was surrounded by in the Pacific Northwest or even the shadowy pine green I encountered in the mountains. When you weave all these hues together with the splashes of color from the flowers growing in Butchart Gardens, you have a magnificent tapestry by none other than the most famous artist of all, Mother Nature.

According to the map, I will be riding 119 miles. The bike route takes a different route than Highway #101 and I will have to ride inland, which will take me uphill until I turn back toward the coast and Santa Barbara. I reach Lom Poc, an oasis of a city. Its economy is based on the large federal prison and Brandenburg Air Force Base. It was now 12:10 p.m. and I am fifty miles into the day. I realize that I am making record time because of the downhill sprints after each climb. I finally hit the last climb twenty-five miles out of Lom Poc and, for the next seven miles, I reach speeds of forty-five-and-a-half MPH going down to the coast.

The signs I have been whizzing by along the way finally register in my mind that I have forty more miles still to go. I had planned on camping fifteen miles south of Santa Barbara. I finally pedal into this beautiful little town at 4 p.m. I have a frozen yogurt for lunch. I casually follow the bike route, which takes me right through town. I am just at State Street when another spoke pops and the wheel goes out of round again before I can stop.

A friendly biker, who stops to offer some assistance, directs me to a bike shop, which is located across the street from the Amtrak station. Since it is already 5:15 p.m., I am pleased that I am able to convince the mechanics at the shop to fix the bike today. While they go to work on the bike, they share a few stories about some robberies that have occurred at the campground I am headed for.

Before I decide what my next plan will be, I wander over to Amtrak to see their schedule and rates to Palm Springs. I know that things happen for a reason. I am relieved to have found this option. My friend, Dan Purgett, was not going to be able to pick me up in Newport as he had originally offered and I would have had to bike through all the Los Angeles traffic and LA runs forever.

The Amtrak office tells me that I can send my bike to Denver, my final destination, from here. I call Greyhound and find connections to Palm Springs leaving in forty-five minutes for $28. I compare the Amtrak fare of $57 leaving at 4 p.m. the next day and schedule the Greyhound offer. I quickly make a decision and grab the bike. I proceed to repack my gear, break down the bike, box and check it in and run nine blocks up the hill to the bus station, carrying my seventy pound pack. I actually make it to the station with sweat dripping from my bike clothes with the bus leaving in two minutes.

I change clothes on the bus and, when the bus stops in Oxnard, I have a chance to wash up in the station. My bus goes to Indio, twenty minutes past Palm Springs, but gets me out of the Los Angeles station which is located in a rough section of downtown. At least the facilities are clean and a small deli restaurant is available. I clean up some more and call Purgett to see if he can meet me when I arrive in Indio at 7 a.m.

Now that I am settled on the bus, I come face to face with reality: my bicycle journey has come to an end.

RECOVERING AND REUNITING

fifteen

With my heart and mind heavy with mixed emotions, I board the Greyhound bus in Santa Barbara. After a fitful night's sleep, I arrive in Indio, California, at 7:20 a.m. I know I am not ready to fully embrace my past or the future, so I figure I will try to extend this last leg of my journey and take a few weeks to try and figure things out.

Dan Purgett, my old friend from Vail, is waiting at the bus station with a friendly grin on his face. He helps me drag the weathered panniers to his car. He has many questions about my journey so I tell him a few stories over the next half hour and he lets me know that my adventure is a feat he admires. We talk about our last meeting a few years ago when he was living in an apartment in one of the small towns along the coast of Southern California. At that time, I had left Vail and was looking for a new location and perhaps a new job in the restaurant business. This never panned out for me so I headed to the Virgin Islands with an offer of a place to stay on the Island of St. John where I eventually got back into the construction business. Dan let me know that the decision for him to move to Palm Springs was based on his passion for the game of golf. I can understand as I see a golf course on every corner as we get closer and closer to his house.

We pull up to his ranch-style house and he gives me a tour of the place. From the looks of the elegant, but practical furniture, Dan seems to have grown a bit more conservative than I remember from the days when we were buddies in Vail. The first thing I expected to see was a large E-Z Boy recliner with all the side compartments. He had one of these at his apartment in Vail when I first met him and he was known for hibernating on or close to the recliner for days at a time. The side pockets and cup holders were always stocked with his essential paraphernalia, including remains of a MacDonald meal close at hand. I recall that I was not the only friend whom he solicited to bring over some sort of fast food when we came over for a visit. After a few days, he would emerge from his *cave* and dive back into his busy world as a builder. In fact, I remember when he built Moe's school, The Learning Tree, while he was in the midst of renovating several other projects in downtown Vail.

As we pass the kitchen, he hands me a bundle of mail. He helps me toss the panniers across the back of the chair in the guest room and lets me know that he will return for cocktail hour after he does a few errands and maybe a round of golf. As he walks out, he says to make myself at home. I glance at the plush bed and know a nap would have to wait. I have mail!. I spot the pool on the other side of the sliding glass door and decide to sit on a lounge in the shade and see what the postman delivered.

There is a small package and two letters, and I am anxious to see what intriguing surprise Moe has sent me from Colorado. I decide to open the package first. It contains a book, *Reviving Ophelia* by Mary Pipher. There is a short note inside from Moe saying that before we make our final decision about reuniting, she wants me to read this book about what it is like to be a young girl growing up in today's world of hyper-media pressure. I have never been married, nor do I have any children of my own; my experience with growing up with a teenage sister has always baffled me.

My sister, Georgeanne, had always been very close my brother, Jim, and me until she reached puberty. Then things, as I recall, seemed to change. She no longer wanted to be our buddy and confidant. Our mother was not adept at sharing her feelings and did not educate Jim and me about this sensitive phase in a young girl's life so we just drifted apart. I am more than willing now to read some information on the subject so that I might be better prepared for possibly becoming part of Moe's family which includes a teenage girl.

I am eager to see what is in the other two letters with postmarks five days apart. I set the book aside and open the first letter. In Moe's way of carefully choosing words, she explains how much she misses me and that, although the growth she continues to make as a single woman inspires her, she realizes that she needs to be part of a couple in order to test her growth as a confident human being. She believes in the *us* part of Moe and Lou and is willing to give our partnership another try.

Ailish is growing up and developing a life of her own. She is investigating colleges, taking college entrance exams, working part-time and involved in a healthy social life at her high school. My absence has given Ailish a chance to see that I am a contributing member of the household which makes her mom's life feel a bit more complete. Perhaps she realizes she, herself, will soon be moving on and wants her mom to be happy. Moe ends the letter explaining the importance of respecting Ailish's place in the family and the need to give her support and space to grow into a healthy young woman.

Moe has always been, and will always be, an educator. I can now see why she sent the book, *Reviving Ophelia*. She knew its contents would reveal an important lesson for me. At this moment in time, she is not asking for any long-term commitment, only that we explore each day together to see how life unfolds.

I figure that I better open the third envelope before I am able to put all the pieces of this puzzle together. To my surprise, it included two things: a picture of Moe, Ailish and me, together and an invitation to join them, along with Ailish's girlfriend, Ryan, in Playa del Carmen, Mexico for a pre-Christmas vacation. Perhaps this will give all of us a chance to get to know one another as individuals on neutral territory.

Ailish had made friends with a young man who worked at the hotel in Mexico. Moe had taken Ailish and Ryan there last summer. Ailish was anxious to rekindle this friendship. Ryan was her faithful friend and was like a second daughter to Moe; and I would be Moe's suitemate. The trip is to take place the 19th until the 24th of December, a little more than a month away. I wonder if I should call her tonight, or do I need more time to contemplate the words of her letter? No! My heart tells me that there is no question about my answer. Yes!

I put my feet in the pool and notice that my entire body is aching and exhausted. I lie on the raft and float in the pool until Dan returns for cocktail hour. He has brought a girlfriend back to the house. The three of us drink through the dinner hour. I can clearly see that she is important to him, but it does not seem to be a two-way street.

Later that night when I am lying in bed, I am struck by the fact that I want way more than a superficial relationship. I think I have grown on my bike journey. I am able to see how casually the young woman handles Dan's feelings and attempts at intimacy. I recognize that I have had way too many of those kinds of relationships myself. Somehow, I recognize that there was never any doubt in my mind that I would be returning to Colorado.

On my bike trip, I visited the homes of old friends whom I used to party with in my youth. They all now appear to be grounded in solid partnerships. I was able to see how they handled everyday life with the ups and downs that accompany working and playing as a family unit. I wonder if it is not too late to see myself in this role.

The next few days come and go. I find myself regaining strength and renewed energy. I finish the book Moe sent and we talk several times on the phone about being back together and a new perspective about the role each of us might play in the family. She has been talking to Ailish about my return. Ailish has finally found a place for me in her heart and is ready to welcome me to their home. I let Moe know that I respect and am aware of how involved she is in managing and teaching at Learning Tree and Colorado Mountain College, a career she can't put on hold as we launch into a romance. Moe and I both agree that this leap into uncertainty is both terrifying and exciting. I have a feeling we will land on solid ground and will never again let go of one another.

The next day, I book a train ticket to Glenwood Springs, Colorado, where Moe has offered to meet me the next weekend. My bike, which was shipped to Denver, will be waiting for me to pick up at the train station before the end of the month. Moe tells me that it has started to snow already in the mountains so it will be a while before I am able to get in the saddle of my Jamison Coda for a long ride.

Our reunion in Glenwood Springs is warm, in spite of the chilly temperatures that have settled into the mountains. As we drive to Vail to begin a new chapter in our lives, I chatter on with stories from my trip and express with all my heart that I want to return to the Pacific Northwest, but this time, to share the beauty of it together.

sixteen

As I was pedaling one mile at a time, one more hill or one more curve, I thought to myself, "I'll be there if I just keep turning these wheels." At times, I thought I was isolated from the world and, in reality, I think that I became more a part of it on that journey of a lifetime when I was turning fifty.

Soon I am living a new dream, one I would not have imagined three months ago when I embarked on my long-distance bike trip.

Ailish and Moe welcome me into their lives and, as seamlessly as possible, the three of us resume our life together in Vail. The upcoming trip to Mexico makes a perfect transition. The days blend together and create a collage of overlapping memories.

Ailish graduates from high school and begins a new chapter of her life as a student at Colorado State University, where she eventually meets Richard, the love of her life.

Moe continues teaching young children at Learning Tree and the teachers who nurture them at Colorado Mountain College for five more years when the school closes its doors for the last time on the night we leave for Galveston, Texas to prepare for our wedding.

I decide to open a new business based on my past experience over the years in Vail, Aspen and St John, USVI. During the three years I spent in St. John, I had done a dozen home remodels and over the years in the mountains, I had done quite a few restaurant remodels and construction jobs in between starting other business ventures throughout my adult life.

My first job, after returning to the Vail Valley, is the biggest and the most exciting of my career. I rebuild a ninety-five-year-old home in Eagle and transform it into a beautiful Georgia-Victorian. My interior design work for restaurants and homes, along with my fine-tuned electrical and plumbing skills and the creative waterfalls I built at Moe's house, all give me the necessary background to engage in some challenging projects. My new company will do home repairs, remodels and landscape architecture, based around water features.

Moe and I squeeze in vacations that take us to four different continents, and begin to build dreams for our future together.

When I tuck away the journals and photos from my bike trip, little do I know I will be taking them out of the white box thirteen years later so that Moe can transcribe them into a book.

SEVEN YEARS LATER:
THE WEDDING

seventeen

"Let me tell the next part of our story, Lou."

It had taken seven years after you returned from your *quest*, for us to feel we were ready for the next step. We had fallen in love with Mexico, as well as each other. At first, we planned to celebrate our wedding there, but chose another beautiful beach closer to those who wanted to share our happiness. On May 25, 2002, Lou and I gathered with our dearest family and friends on the beach in Galveston, Texas, where we released live butterflies as a symbol of a new beginning and shared the vows we wrote to one another. The sea and the world around us has been a passion for us as a couple so we concluded our wedding ceremony with an exchange of gifts of nature and these words, while all the while one of the released butterflies sat perched on Lou's shirt pocket over his heart.

"Lou, you came softly and slowly into my life. Because you love me, I see with new eyes and hear with new ears. I delight in everyday and in every adventure we share. I want to give you a gift of nature, a piece of beach glass. It is a symbol of how my life has changed. Like the beautiful colored glass, we are tumbled by the waves, rubbed together on the sand, bleached in the sun and our edges smoothed out by the abrasion and pleasure of being together."

"Moe, our love grew slowly; it started with a true friendship and blossomed to what it is today. Your love gives me strength and courage as we face our future together with optimism and joy. I want to give you a gift from the sea, a heart-shaped shell found on beaches we have traveled on together. It is a symbol of my love for you."

The wedding celebration continued for the rest of the week before we returned home to Vail to begin our life as a newly married couple. We took with us a bundle of memories tucked into our wedding album to remind us of this commitment to one another.

One evening when we were finishing up our day, Lou asked, "Hey, Moe, do you mind if I take one of the wedding photos and add it to my white memory box?"

I nodded, delighted to be a part of Lou's life treasures, tucked neatly away in the back of the upstairs closet. Little did I know that this box of treasures would be pulled out again so soon and packed up when we sold the house and moved to Mexico a few months later.

From the day Lou pedaled off from my arms in Steamboat Springs, Colorado, in 1995 on his two-and-a-half-month-long bike journey, he knew he wanted to show me the beauty that abounds in the west, along the Puget Sound in particular.

I arrived home one sunny summer day in 2002 to the joyous announcement that Lou could not wait any longer to take me to the Pacific Northwest to relive a portion of his bicycle journey. "I couldn't resist, Moe; I found a good deal and booked two plane tickets to Seattle. We won't need to buy a travel guide; we'll use my journals."

Bubbling over with excitement, I responded, "When should I start packing? I'm only joking, I know I will have to wait a few weeks until our departure day arrives, but just so you know, I can be ready at a moment's notice."

During the next month, life as a married couple was filled with conversations that included our hopes and dreams for the future. From one of our earliest back-door-tour trips to Costa Rica, we had talked about buying property south of the border and creating some sort of small tourist-related business where we could carve out a living and immerse ourselves in a more peaceful, affordable lifestyle of retirement than we knew was possible in Vail, Colorado, which we called home.

"Do you think this dream will ever become a reality?" I asked one evening as we sat beside the fire pit on the sandy beach Lou had created in our garden in Vail.

"Moe, if we are really serious about this dream, then we can start now to look for a location. I have been reading that the Australian government is offering tax breaks to people who will settle and start businesses in Tasmania. It is an island and you have your Irish-Australian Durack relatives who live near Perth whom you want to meet. What do you think of this idea?" I know my face was projecting a bit of a grimace when he looked to me for a response. "I'm excited that you want to actually explore this dream, but I was imagining a location a bit closer to home."

I continued, "I have only one daughter. One day she and Rich may have children, and I know I don't want to be so far away. Maybe we could begin our search in Mexico?" For just a moment, I recalled the full-moon evening on the beach in Galveston, Texas, the night after our wedding, when Ailish came walking toward us with tears in her eyes and an outstretched hand announcing that Rich had asked her to marry him, and she said, "yes"!

Lou took the lead and began to research the possibilities in the Yucatan Peninsula of Mexico, where we had vacationed often, the last few years. This vision began to develop into a plan that just might grow into what both of us had in mind for the next chapter of our lives.

"Hey, Moe, perhaps it is time to begin the search for a piece of property on which to build this dream. I think we need to postpone the trip to the Pacific Northwest and follow the momentum that seems to be growing to retire south of the border."

I knew how much Lou wanted to share a piece of his past with me by backtracking on the same roads he pedaled on his Jamison Coda in 1995, but I agreed with him that the other option felt like a priority.

We did find that piece of paradise on Tulum beach, only one mile south of the unforgettable Tulum ruins. One year later, we sold our house and closed one door of our life in the ski resort of Vail, Colorado. We drove south to Mexico in a used Suburban, pulling a trailer with 4,000 pounds of our belongings which we could not sell, give away or bear to part with. This adventurous move to the Riviera Maya proved to be a roller coaster ride. We documented the journey along what we called *the Mariposa Trail*. I transcribed the journals and eventually published the book, <u>*Embarking on the Mariposa Trail,*</u> spilling all the secrets we had uncovered on our journey.

Yes, leaping into uncertainty was terrifying, but I knew in my heart that we would land on solid ground and never let go of one another.

Over the next few years, our dream of owning and operating a B & B south of the border became a reality. We learned a lesson about dreams; if you let go of one, you just might find a better one waiting for you around a corner. This is exactly what happened. When we realized we could not get permits to build what we wanted on the beach; perhaps the jungle, just a few miles inland, would provide just such an oasis for this shift in thinking. We found a buyer for the beach lot and expanded the property we were living on in a small Mayan pueblo, Macario Gomez, only twelve miles from the popular tourist Mecca of Tulum.

At *La Selva Mariposa*, The Jungle Butterfly, we slowly added a room or two at a time and built up a reputation for *an elegant boutique hotel*

that is operated by a couple from Colorado who share a passion for their new home and the surrounding countryside.

Lou and I blossomed under the gentle guidance of the *mariposas* (butterflies) that frequented our waterfalls, *cenote-style* pools and gardens, lush with tropical plants and flowers. We often reflected on these familiar words, "In order to be happy one needs three important things: something to do, someone to love and something to look forward to."

We had each other and we were never at a loss for something to do. Lou's carpentry and design skills expanded in this environment, abundant in tropical hard wood, natural limestone, eager laborers and unlimited time. Lou and his crew of Mayan workers finished the fourth suite with its own pool and waterfall at *La Selva Mariposa* and it was fit for a Mayan king. Each piece of limestone was hand-hewn and carefully put in place. The detail on the *casita* was inspired by the ancient architects who created the ruined cities of Ek Balam, Tulum and Coba'. The art that was incorporated in both the interior and exterior of the three-room suite was carved by a Mayan, named Regulo, from the nearby pueblo of Manuel Antonio Hay. Lou had a vision for each room in the suite and the final results, furnished with textiles from our road trips in Mexico, was spectacular.

You might have thought that Lou would now stop to rest, but there was always one more creative idea to bring to fruition; like the spa, a waterfall and a bubbling-reflection stream which connected the spa to the magnificent Chichen Itza waterfall and pond in front of our house.

Were our days of travel over now that we were inn keepers of a successful B & B, and had a grandchild living in Colorado? Was wanderlust a thing of the past?

Neither of us wanted to admit that we were getting older and settling into this paradise in the jungle with ease and comfort, but that Jamison Coda still sat beside Lou's workshop, reminding us daily of his long past adventure to the Pacific Northwest and our plans to return one day.

THE THIRD THING

eighteen

September and October are the rainy months in the Yucatan Peninsula and we decided in 2009 to just close *La Selva Mariposa* and return to the states to visit our friends and family in Colorado during this down time for innkeepers. "Why don't we preface our time to Colorado with a trip to San Juan Islands and Vancouver?" I suggested, while lazing under a *palapa* on the beach. "We've been putting off that journey for much too long."

"Yes!" Lou said. "That's it - the third thing: something to look forward to!"

With no guests or reservations to keep us busy the last two weeks of August because of the swine flu scare that spring, we impulsively decided to look for flights to Seattle and leave a little early. Julio, our key employee and his wife and young child, agreed to stay at *La Selva Mariposa* to take care of the property and our three dogs while we were away.

The speed with which the travel plans were moving forward created added excitement and a bit of stress, knowing we would be away for over two months. Lou did a little research on hotels in key places we would visit. We had hoped, because of lower prices, to be visiting this popular tourist destination in the off-season, but to our dismay, low season in the Pacific Northwest doesn't begin until mid-October.

The tickets were purchased; there was no turning back. We reminded each other that this was an important vacation for us for several reasons: to relive the highlights of Lou's bicycle trip of 1995, to create new memories and to treat ourselves after a busy tourist season at *La Selva Mariposa*.

"Ok," I said. "We don't need to stay at the Empress Hotel in Victoria or the Rosario Resort on Orcas Island, but we have to revisit your favorite locations and try to include a few bike rides, even though the Jamison Coda will not be coming along."

Good friends, who are also hotel/villa owners in Mexico, had recently moved to the wine country in the state of Washington and invited us to visit them the first week of our trip. Yes, we would be heading away from our destination; the Puget Sound, but dear friends are worth adding a backdoor tour, and altering our original plans for the trip.

On the first leg of our journey, with a panoramic view of water and bridges below us, we arrive at the Seattle airport before noon and book two seats on a bus to Prosser, a few hours away. The drive east on I-90, away from the jagged coastline, gives us some spectacular views of Mt. Rainer, standing at 14,410 feet. This spectacle is surrounded by glaciers and rich green pine forests whose trees seem to be hanging onto the steep slopes in the distance. We notice that the familiar Colorado pine-beetle-kill is not evident in the mountain landscape whizzing past our window. I overhear the guy in front of us say, "Look, honey, the mountain is out!" In other words, we are presented with an unusually clear Pacific Northwest day, and are temporarily blinded by the reflection of the snow in the bus window.

I begin to look at a travel brochure about the state of Washington and doze off while reading about its birth during a time when the State slept under the sea. As the tectonic plates lifted the Evergreen State out of the waters, the area was covered in basalt lava, the thickness of pancake syrup. Normal erosion hardly made a dent in it, but the flowing glacier waters, accompanied by fierce wind, did change the landscape, leaving behind an area rich in black dirt, pencil-thin waterfalls and dramatic mountain vistas. As I wake I wonder, "Could what I read be correct? Maybe I should read the brochure again, or not?"

We arrive in Prosser, the birthplace of the Washington State wine industry, and are warmly greeted by our friends, Sherry and Jeff, who are eager to show us their new home and surrounding countryside. As we drive around with them, it is easy to see that this part of Washington's economy centers around agriculture: wine grapes, apples, cherries, hops, asparagus, corn and wheat.

This scenic area is surrounded by hills with names like Horsehaven and Rattlesnake, bisected by the Yakima River running through it like a snake on the move. We stop for a delicious lunch and wine tasting at the Olsen Estates and catch up on our lives while dining beside a flowing fountain in the courtyard. Afterwards, we proceed to Thurston Wolfe, followed by Vinehart Wineries, both or which feature quaint little tasting venues and a sampling of food to complement our wine choices.

Sherry and Jeff bring up the fact that we left the Yucatan because it is our rainiest season there but we will soon be traveling along the coastal areas of the Pacific Northwest, known for abundant rainfall.

I slip in my two cents worth and mention casually, "Do you guys remember the *chipi-chipi rain* along the Riviera Maya that softy drizzles down as you go about your life without even a pause?"

Sherry responds, "Yes, Moe, but it was those thunder-blasting storms, accompanied by an amazing lightening display, which made me cringe and wonder if our *palapa* roof was going to catch on fire."

Lou adds, "The winds were the thing that always scared me during one of those hurricane-force storms. Our trees are not firmly rooted in the ground, because of the rocky limestone soil and, after watching, over fifty good-size trees tumble during hurricane Emily, I knew our trees were fragile."

My favorite vision during one of these drenching storms was of the tropical plants, flowers and trees joyously singing as they soaked up each drop of rainwater. There is nothing like rain to make a garden blossom and grow.

I am thinking out loud when I say that perhaps we will be able to make a comparison between the tropical storms and the well-known rain of the Pacific Northwest when Lou says, "Moe, I am hoping that sunny skies follow us until we return to the airport in Seattle. I know I lucked out on my bike trip as there were no showers the first few weeks, but the one day I rode for four hours in rain was really my worst day, mostly because you miss all the beauty which lies around you because you have to be so intensely focused on the road - no easy task."

As we talk about our upcoming trip to the Pacific coast, Sherry and Jeff tell us about their recent road trip to the San Juan Islands and the Olympic Peninsula. They traveled in their car because they wanted to bring their dog, Chloe, but found that they wasted a lot of time and money by not using more of the available public transportation.

They ask if there is any improvement with public transportation in the Riviera Maya since they left a few years ago. I respond to their question, "As long as you are staying in one of the hotels or towns along the main highway from Cancun to Tulum and south, there are buses, vans, and taxis, but as soon as you veer off Highway #307, your options are still very limited. There is talk of a rail system from Cancun to Tulum, and a new van service inland from Tulum to Valladolid, but as long as the taxi company retains control of the transportation monopoly in the area, change will be very slow, in a place where slow is the norm." Since both of us have hotels off the main strip, we agree that our guests are still better off renting a car than depending on public transportation at this time.

TRAVELING IN TANDEM

nineteen

It is time to begin our journey back to the coast and relive the days Lou spent one fall more than ten years ago. He knows he will be seeing the Pacific Northwest with new eyes.

"Moe, this feels like a dream come true. You can't imagine how many times on my bicycle journey I said, "If only Moe were here," or "I want to come back here one day and show this area of the world to Moe."

"Lou, I actually can imagine it. Have you forgotten that I transcribed your travel journals and you did say those exact words many times along the way? I feel like the one who is living a dream. I can't believe, with all we have been through, —moving from Colorado to Mexico and building and operating our Bed and Breakfast - that we are finally making this trip."

I am deep in thought at the moment, recalling an earlier trip when we bought a few bottles of wine right before we drove across the Mexican border. We could not uncork the bottle until we had almost reached our final destination, Tulum, because we did not bring a cork screw along and could not find one in any of the small towns where we spent the night. Well, I have a wine opener in my backpack this time, and a nice bottle of red we bought at one of the friendly wineries Jeff and Sherry took us to near Prosser. Maybe we will open it tonight to celebrate the start of our journey.

We say *adios* to our friends and board a coach to Anacortes,

167

Washington, with a change of buses at the Seattle airport. While on the bus, we engage in some planning for the next few days ahead and decide we will have to see the majority of the San Juan Islands, except Vancouver Island, from a ferry because high-season prices and no vacancies at affordable B & B venues leave us little choice. "Maybe it wasn't such a good idea after all to travel in August and early September," I added.

"It is what it is," said Lou. "Let's not think any more about it and enjoy every minute of the trip."

Our first encounters with public transportation in the Pacific Northwest turn out to be pleasant ones. The buses are inexpensive, convenient and work well with the airport connections, as well as the train and ferry systems in the area. This way of traveling gives us plenty of time to relax and plan for the future and, most of all, feel the love we share at this moment in time.

When we first planned to re-visit the Pacific Northwest, it was just after we married and now, seven years later, our relationship has grown as we encounter the *topes* (speed bumps) life has tossed in our path. We originally planned to build and operate a Bed and Breakfast on the property we purchased on Tulum beach, but the Mexican government made it impossible to get permits to build what we wanted. We were able to sell our beach property before it was re-zoned to national park. To this day, nothing has been built on *our* lot and Mother Nature continues to reclaim her share of the ground little by little, even though no significant hurricanes have blown up the Caribbean coast since the sale. We used to laugh about the property across the street being beachfront one day and within a decade this could become a reality.

Both Lou and I are drawn to the sea when we go on vacation and yet we live fifteen minutes from the most beautiful sugar-sand beaches in the world bordering the turquoise waters of the Caribbean. I find that the wind, waves and sun at the beach recharge my creative energy sources and I feel calm when I return to our little oasis in the jungle. Yes, somehow we have managed to carve out a life which includes the best of both worlds; the beach and the jungle.

When we travel, we are constantly researching how we can improve our Bed and Breakfast/boutique hotel and serve our clients better. Our to-do list always seems to be created somewhere along the way and is pulled out of our pocket as soon as we return home. There's nothing better than checking off items from your list as you walk around your property and see reflections of your hard work and dreams blossoming before you.

Enough of the past; it is now time to focus on our bus ride back to the sea which presents vistas of green with high mountains looming in the distance. Lou and I are both thrilled to finally see the emerald water of the Puget Sound in the distance. Let the adventure begin!

We let the bus driver know where we are staying in Anacortes and he pulls into the hotel parking lot to drop us off at the door. The receptionist offers us freshly baked cookies, which we take to our room, down a rather dreary hallway. To our disappointment, we only have a view of the parking lot and we are miles from the center of town and the ferry docks. So much for booking a mid-priced hotel online; but we both recall a time when we were hauling the trailer on our move from Colorado to Tulum, Mexico. On that journey along the *Mariposa Trail,* we only stayed at hotels that gave us a view of the parking lot so that we could keep an eye on what remained of our worldly belongings.

We see no taxis in sight, so we begin to walk into town to see what has changed in Anacortes since Lou's trip and what it has to offer in terms of restaurants and green spaces. Lou's journal has high marks for this little town so we don't want to miss anything. This is one time we would not have minded paying an expensive taxi fare as a chill is in the air. We are getting close to the water and we notice how the winds are picking up. We don't see signs of the fishing or boat building industry until we reach the marina at Sunset Beach. Glancing across Rosario Strait at the San Juan Islands, we admire the moored boats and let our imaginations go with thoughts of what it might be like to explore the area on a luxury chartered yacht or sail boat. Where is the *Lui-Nu* when you need her?

It is Sunday night so many of the restaurants and the famous marine supply and hardware stores are closed. How much fun it would have been to explore the oldest marine hardware store on the west coast! Maybe we would have picked up some plumbing fittings or other essential hardware, but, on second thought, perhaps it is best that it is closed, as there is little room left in our one small suitcase on wheels and an assortment of backpacks and tote bags.

"Lou, I was wondering how you knew just what to buy on those many trips to Lowe's Home Depot and Ace Hardware when we were preparing to move to Mexico and build our *casa* there?"

"If you remember, Moe, I went down to Mexico for a couple of weeks the spring before we moved to remodel Victor's little beach shack and add a kitchen and shower so that it would be more comfortable for us when we moved the next October. I found out first hand just how hard it was to find fittings and parts for plumbing work. It was just like building thirty-five years ago in Vail, when you had to go into stores and look to see what was on the shelves and then figure out a way to jury-rig, or invent a new way to use the materials at hand. I saw just how little was available and how many stores you had to go to in order to find one part. As far as shopping for our *casa* on the beach, I had completed plans including plumbing and electrical, so I had an idea of what I would need. I filled half-dozen large plastic containers with plumbing and electrical pieces which I am actually still using today."

"I know I always tease you about visiting the little Mayan gal at the hardware store in Francisco Uh May, but you do take a lot of trips there when you are doing a project at *La Selva Mariposa*."

"Well, I like to shop locally when I can and the little hardware store in the next *pueblo* is actually a pretty good resource for me. Moe, you know I only have eyes for you."

I smiled at Lou and said, "To change the subject back to our luggage, Honey. That was such a great idea to ship our big duffle bag with extra clothing to Rich and Ailish's house in Colorado. I'm not so sure we would have enjoyed schlepping that one off and on ferries and buses."

"Thanks for the acknowledgement. I told you I was a seasoned traveler in these parts," Lou said.

The most unique things about Anacortes, beside being one of the best jumping off places for the San Juan Islands, is the way the town fathers have chosen to tell the history of this little town. There are over fifty life-size, brightly painted wooden cutouts of the town's forefathers engaged in their daily work as fishermen, boat builders, bakers, carpenters, school teachers and shop owners. These wooden sculptures are mounted on the fronts and sides of all the buildings in town. As we walk the two and a half miles after dinner back to our hotel, we get a glimpse of days-gone-by in Anacortes, Washington.

While falling asleep, I reflect that we are only eighty-five miles from Seattle. This distance is multiplied many times by the serenity I already feel while snuggled in a warm bed knowing we will be crossing the dark-green waters in just a few hours.

The next morning, the hotel receptionist calls a cab to takes us to the Washington State ferry dock. Our cab driver enlightens us to the fact that the thick mist of marine air is typical and will lift by nine, but Lou already knew that bit of weather information. The temperature of fifty-four degrees lets us know that fall is in the air. When we reach the dock, we can see flocks of frigate birds and sea gulls. We purchase our tickets and are ushered frantically onto the Chalan ferry as if it is departing momentarily for Sydney Harbor.

The Washington State fleet of ferry boats varies in size and age, but all that we travel on are comfortable, clean, never crowded and they provide a very relaxing way to see the Pacific Northwest. Perhaps because it is so early in the morning or late in the season, there are only about thirty passengers on this immense vessel. Lou spots a middle-age man who is riding a bike decked up with panniers and goes over to chat with him about his journey. I can hear a bit of envy in Lou's voice when he returns to his seat next to me.

"Lou, I was just thinking about how you used to ride the Jamison Coda a lot during our first spring living in Macario Gomez, but now your prize rig is rarely taken out on a long ride."

"True. That first spring and early summer when we finished building the house, I had time and wanted to get back into the saddle so I tried riding on different days and found that Sunday was the only one that seemed safe and peaceful enough to explore my new neighborhood. The Coba' Road was in terrible shape back then and the taxis and tour buses going to the ruins or to Tulum, in the other direction, made the ride less than safe or enjoyable. After cycling many times to Tulum for coffee and back home or to Coba' for a swim, the ride got boring and the pavement was unbearably hot as summer rolled in."

"That makes sense; I remember that I wouldn't even drive the Coba' road in our huge GMC car during that time because the road was so dangerous."

"When I travel back to Colorado each year, it becomes very clear to me that bike riding is more than exercise or a form of active transportation. Instead, it is time spent in one beautiful site or another. Moe, you will soon see why I loved riding my bike in the Pacific Northwest and along the Pacific coastline."

Yes, we are finally surrounded by water, but the heavy fog prevents us from seeing the emerald isles. Within the first half hour of departure, the captain looses sight on his radar of another ship he knows is also crossing the narrow Rosario Strait so he backs up a couple of miles until he is sure that he is out of range of the other boat. It is easy to see why ships are not always true to the posted schedule.

While watching this fiasco, I say, "Lou does all this water and the name Rosario bring back any memories from our early days in Mexico?"

"Moe, how could I forget the night we took the representative from the notary's office to Filipe Carrillo Puerto to get Rosario Tum Pacab (the teacher whose name would appear on the title) to sign the Power of Attorney, once for all, giving us the needed title document to our beach property once it was released."

"Lou, do you remember how the streets were flooded, the skies alarmingly dark and Rosario's living room even darker?"

"Yes, I recall the rain and that there was a baby sleeping in a hammock in Rosario's living room so they did not turn on any lights."

"I can't forget how scared I was, Lou, because she was taking so long to read over the documents. I was afraid that she would not sign the papers. When the notary's representative asked to see her identification, she was gone for the longest time. All we could hear was the sound of drawers opening and shutting and the movement of objects in the back room. When she did place her signature on the final page, we scooted out the door. Once in the car, our friend, Eli, who had come along to be our translator, noticed that the notary's currier did not have her sign every page, only the last one. We all agreed this was necessary so Lou went back to get the additional signatures. I felt she wanted us to go away and never come back."

"Yes, Moe, but the children's books you brought along for her kindergarten class came in handy for this last push to get closer to making that tiny piece of land ours."

"Well, Lou, I am glad that chapter of our life is over and the whole story recorded in *Embarking on the Mariposa Trail.*

"Looks like our Captain has finally worked through his problem navigating this Rosario," Lou said.

twenty

Well, after our big ordeal crossing the border when we moved from the United States to Mexico, this crossing to Canada seems uneventful. We arrive at the ferry dock at Sydney Harbor, show our passports and walk a block to the tourist office to check out our options for continuing our journey to Victoria and Butchart Gardens. We are in luck, as the young woman behind the desk advises us that for a few bucks, we can take a local bus which will pass by Butchart Gardens. We can get out there, deposit our bags in a safe storage area and tour the gardens for as long as we desire before catching another bus to take us to downtown Victoria where we have made hotel reservations for the next two nights. This turns out to be a perfect plan for the day.

We begin traveling in tandem with another couple our age from Montana: ferry boat, tourist office, Quizno's, bus stop and, finally, the four of us arrive at Butchart Gardens. Greg has a dry sense of humor, just like Lou's and Terry's smile is contagious. Striking up a conversation with them is easy. We laugh at some of their stories about traveling in their RV, and they want us to tell them more about our experiences moving to Mexico. Lou once again takes on the role of a storyteller. He transports us back in time to the border crossing between Laredo, Texas and Nuevo Laredo, Mexico.

"With the winds of winter at our back, we left our home state of Colorado to embark on a journey that led us south of the border. We were chasing our dream to build a B & B perched high above the white sand beach and turquoise waters on our newly purchased property in Tulum. We had prepared for over a year for this step of the journey and were now approaching the Rio Grande Bridge for the border crossing. We paid the toll for our car and trailer, but we did not realize that we needed to wait for a receipt before proceeding to the random red light/ green light check station. We crossed without a hitch when the green light signaled our good news. We headed to the vehicle registration complex. With butterflies in our stomach, we got in line and waited our turn at the window where two Mexicans, who spoke no English, examined our paperwork. We could tell by the way they kept shaking their heads as they examined our documents that something was not right. The gentleman behind us stepped forward to interpret when he saw the confused looks on our faces. They were trying to tell us to go to another building a quarter of a mile away. In this building, the man in charge told us that our FM3 documents had expired. He instructed us to go to the Mexican Consulate on the US side of the river. We had secured our documents at the consulate offices in Denver where we were told that they were good for one year. The clerk there neglected to tell us that they had to be stamped at the border within ninety days to be valid. In fact, he told us not to get them stamped until we were bringing our belongings into Mexico because the first time was the only time you could do this.

We left the car and trailer and walked across the bridge to the consulate office where a secretary there told us that the FM3s were indeed expired and could not be reissued. She continued with, "You are welcome to drive into Mexico using your passports, but you have lost the right to ever bring your household belongings in."

We asked to see the Consulate General and, after relating our story to him, we were again told "no". We pleaded for help and he said he would make a phone call to Denver. Ten minutes later the secretary returned and told us that the Consulate General would reissue our FM3s and stamp our inventory list of household goods if we had everything in order by 9 a.m. tomorrow morning. She also mentioned that we should hurry back to our car, as it was not safe in the vehicle registration parking lot. We rapidly departed the office and vaguely heard her mummer something about needing a customs broker to bring our goods into Mexico.

We saw no taxis, so we hoofed it across the bridge and through the gauntlet to where we had left our vehicles. With a sigh of relief, we saw that all was well so we drove back to the border. When we approached the US customs station, they asked to see the receipt of when we entered Mexico. We told them that we had just entered a few hours ago and never received one. They asked us to open the trailer, and were amazed at what we were trying to bring into the United States. They asked us to pull into a check station where they would examine our vehicles more thoroughly. Before we could move, an ambulance came roaring up and needed access so the guard signaled for us to proceed across the bridge in order to clear the area. Sometimes you get lucky!

We checked into a hotel on a back street and asked for a room with a view of our car and trailer, of course. We began the task of calling our banks in Colorado where we had recently closed our accounts. The new bank account we had just opened in Ft. Collins, where our daughter lives, would not have the history we needed. Because we were getting retirement FM3 documents, we had to prove that we had a $1,500 monthly income in the states. We were instructed to retype the list of our household items because I had added things we had purchased along the way. The list, in Spanish, could have no crossovers or add-ons; it had to be perfect. The hotel proprietors let us use their computer to rewrite the inventory list and their fax for receiving letters from our banks. After making all the necessary copies, the task was complete.

At 9 a.m. the following morning, we took our documents back to the Consulate and were amazed when they told us to return at 1 p.m. to pick up our visas and stamped inventory list. The secretary asked if we had called a customs broker. We told her that we had called one yesterday. The broker told us to bring our stamped letter and she would take care of paying the required fees. I asked her many questions and still it was unclear as to what exactly a customs broker's job entailed.

We returned as requested at 1 p.m. and picked up our prepared documents. We were anxious to get started on our trip so we decided to see what would happen if we just skipped the customs broker part and proceeded across the bridge. This time we got the receipt after paying the toll and passing the red light. The attendant waved us into a check-in area under a carport. He asked us to open the car and trailer, and immediately said, "This needs to go through a customs broker." After some discussion, the custom's agent smiled and said, "You are my *amigo*, today and only today, I will let you go." PS: He did not ask for any money for this favor.

Before anyone could change his/her mind, we drove off to the vehicle registration area with huge smiles on our faces. We found ourselves in the same line, with the same attendants as yesterday. We proudly handed them our new set of documents. They examined our papers carefully and found yet another problem. The visas on our passport were stamped Oct. 26th and this was Oct. 24th. After much conversation using our best Spanish, they agreed that it was indeed a sloppy mistake by the Consulate. They took our fingerprints and sent us to the next line to pay the nominal fee for the vehicle registration sticker. They had no interest in our household goods list. Their job concerned only vehicles. We put the sticker on our windshield and headed south.

We had been warned that there was another checkpoint thirty miles from the border, and, if they found anything wrong, they would send us back. We were prepared for the worst. When we approached this checkpoint, we slowed down to two miles an hour and they waved us through. We were on *the mariposa trail* with all the excitement and wonder an adventure like this offers." Lou draws a long breath at the end of his condensed recital of our south of the border experiences.

Back on the bus, our traveling friends look in amazement at both of us as our bus pulls into Butchart Garden's terminal. They let us know they will be taking the fast track tour of the gardens in order to return before dark to their RV parked in a parking lot on the other side of the border. We say good-bye. Lou and I opt for an in depth exploration of the park and each of the magnificent gardens, alive with brilliant shades of red, pink, purple and yellow. At times like this, you can truly appreciate the convenience and difference between the digital camera and the standard variety which Lou had with him on his first trip to Butchart, more than ten years before. We gleefully record hundreds of images in the gorgeous garden.

When Lou stopped here on his bicycle journey, he bought dozens of packets of seeds which we eventually planted in our gardens in Colorado, but with the poor soil and an over-abundance of sunshine, we know that most of the varieties we are viewing will not grow from seed in our gardens in the Yucatan Peninsula of Mexico. We pass right by the gift shop without the usual urge to linger.

We stop to hear a concert near the entrance area. When our senses have been saturated with the sights, sounds, smells and textures of the most abundant and beautiful flowers we had ever seen, we pick up our bags from the free baggage storage area and hop on the next bus to Victoria. We feel like seasoned travelers already. We know that the bus drivers do not make change. We are prepared with the exact fare which we pop into the money slot and settle in for the forty-five-minute bus ride to Victoria.

> On the bus we add a *Note to Self*: "Make a greenhouse at *La Selva Mariposa* for growing flowers." Within minutes we scratch this one off the list and add, "Buy as many flowers of one color as we can to fill our new flower beds now being constructed while we are on vacation."

The bus station in Victoria is only a few blocks from the waterfront. We cannot resist the urge to head to the water where everything begins and ends in the city. We realize our hotel is still a few blocks beyond. An invitation from the Pedi-cab driver to give us a lift, finds us looking at each other simultaneously nodding heads and handing over our luggage.

Upon approaching our hotel, we already feel we are in a new country - one that was once a commonwealth of Great Britain. The lobby is decorated in a Scottish plaid motif and the welcoming staff, with English accents, gets us registered and shows us to our room, which turns out to be more like a one-room apartment with a living room, kitchen, dining nook, bedroom and bath.

It is immediately a toss-up as to whether we want to just crash and enjoy the surroundings or begin our exploration of Victoria. I see some Scottish shortbread cookies and fixings for tea and decide that this is just the thing to get us moving again. Over tea, Lou and I discuss the value of tea time vs. the cocktail hour we are used to in the tropics. Lou told me how he met some English sailors when he was living aboard his boat, the *Lui-Nu*, off St. John, USVI. They swore that a cup of English black tea was just the thing to cool your body down and give you a lift to carry-on long into the night.

The temperature is definitely colder than it has been in Central

Washington where we have spent the last week. We layer up with our warmest clothes and head out to the waterfront. The full moon is not out yet, but the historical government buildings are lit up with thousands of tiny white lights and the stunning Empress Hotel is the pinnacle of interest among the beautiful mixture of old and new buildings lining the shore of the Puget Sound.

As we stroll, we pass a lovely young Irish girl, playing a tune on her violin with the violin case open for donations. We again comment about the European feel of the area, and after dropping some of our newly acquired Canadian money into her case, we walk on. A couple entertainers, who tell the audience they are reinvented lawyers, are just beginning their acrobatic performance entitled, *Beauty, Brawn and Balance*. We take a seat on the garden wall and enjoy the presentation. We are not sure they are able to make the same living they can as lawyers, but we can see they are experiencing joy in this new line of work.

After a snack and a glass of wine at a restaurant on the water, we walk back to our hotel under a full moon. The photo-op of the moon rising over the Empress Hotel is a once-in-a-lifetime-opportunity for us. We stop to take a fair number of snapshots along with a few other tourists, doing the same.

The next day, an old medical problem flares up. I am in need of urgent care so the hotel van driver takes us to one of the national clinics. After a short half-hour wait, I see the clinic doctor and present a letter from my doctor in Mexico. I agree to forgo some tests because of records I have in hand from my *médico*, the Canadian physician writes a prescription. We are pleased with the medical attention I received and the opportunity to see how another country handles health care. We pay the $90 US fee and discover at the pharmacy that they will not fill the prescription without my passport for identification. We casually walk back to our hotel using another route to retrieve it and look at this as an opportunity to see a different part of the city of Victoria.

When the mission is completed, we find a bike rental shop and begin our bike tour of the area at the Bay Convention Center. We are astonished by the flowers in bloom everywhere - in raised gardens, in trees, in hanging baskets. The colors are startlingly bright. Lou, as always, leads me on another of his famous back door tours. We breeze by the inner harbor, pass James Bay Cruise Ship Terminal and, before long, we are in Beacon Hill Park where families with children, young couples and seniors are enjoying the in-and-out sunshine of the afternoon. More than one area has a friendly game of croquet or cricket going. There is a popular walking path which follows the waterfront, but, on our bikes, we stick with the road that weaves through the gardens and past another Totem Park into some old established neighborhoods. The traffic moves at a normal pace; drivers are very respectful of pedestrians and bikers.

It is extraordinary to see that there are many similarities between our new discoveries and the environment which surrounds *La Selva Mariposa* in Mexico. I guess I have always had a fascination with indigenous cultures because their art is influenced by the natural beauty around them and the heavens above. The pre-Columbian Northwest First Nation People used the natural cedar, which was plentiful in the forests where they lived, to build their homes and the totems which told their stories. There was an abundance of natural resources so their lives were relatively easy. They had time to devote to fine arts and crafts and to religious and social ceremonies. At times there was warring among the tribes, but, as a Nation, they never surrendered title to their lands or ceded the power to make decisions within their territory.

The Yucatan Peninsula, where we live, is also in the midst of what was once a sacred space for the ancient Maya during pre-Columbian times. There is evidence that these strong, proud people lived only twenty kilometers from our home in the now abandoned city of Coba' as early as 300 A.D. During the Classic Period, 600 to 900 A.D., the city of Coba' was home to over 55,000 Mayans and thousands more who came from the south to trade their goods.

This trade and cultural exchange with other indigenous groups influenced their art and architecture. Their stories and art were also inspired by nature and the heavens above. Also, like the Pacific Northwest Indians, the Mayans built their pyramids out of abundant material which, in this case, was limestone. Sapling trees were used to build homes for the working-class people who lived outside the sacred city. The Mayans were well known for their writing (an advanced form of hieroglyphics) and their mathematics and astrology. Their artistically decorated temples, pyramids and observatories, built without metal tools, were reclaimed by the jungle when the people mysteriously disappeared from Coba'. The Mayan people never completely disappeared, but most were integrated with the Toltecs, or other indigenous groups. Later, the Spaniards formed a mixed race which makes up almost ninety percent of Mexico's population today. What remains of the pure Mayan people settled in small *pueblos* like the one surrounding *La Selva Mariposa*. Our employees are all Mayan; they speak their ancient language to one another as they joyfully go about their tasks each day. As we look around us at *La Selva Mariposa*, we can see many examples of the art and workmanship of these clever descendents of the pyramid builders.

Busy with my thoughts of ancient artists, I realize that we have approached the Bay Center shopping area. We turn right until we see the enormous decorative arch which signals we are at Chinatown. I recall some of Lou's earlier experiences as we pedal under the arch. We feel this is a good time to dismount, park our bikes and wander along the streets and alleys to experience the flavor of this pocket of the city. Four Asian men are deep in conversation, with Starbuck coffee cups in hand, in front of the popular shop at the entrance of Fan Tan Alley. This street is appropriately named alley as it can fit no more than four people walking side by side, but it has a fascinating array of shops tugging me along. We are reminded of a scene in the movie, *Bird on a Wire*, with Mel Gibson and Goldie Hawn, where they are being chased through a busy, narrow passageway. We walk down the alley, stopping at each shop along the way. I find two matching hats, one for me and one for my grandson, Kaidan, before going back to our bikes.

Criss-crossing through the streets, my eye catches glimpses of lovely shops along the way until we are back at the waterfront. I can't resist taking a photo of a sea gull eating leftovers he found in a bag from the McDonald's chain in a roadside trash can. I wonder if there will ever be a McDonald's Restaurant in our neighborhood of Macario Gomez or the bigger town of Tulum.

We return the bikes and walk back to the hotel. I thank Lou for being such a great tour guide and for sharing some of his favorite memories with me. We decide to stop and have that glass of wine he remembers wishing I could have shared with him many years ago at the Empress Hotel lobby bar. We are disappointed to discover that only registered guests are now allowed in the hotel lobby. Although the tea room with an entrance on the side welcomes visitors, we decide that later this evening we can brew a pot of tea in our little suite at the Scottish inn.

We reminisce about a few of our full moon trips and feel fortunate that we are making this journey down memory lane with the added attraction of *la luna llena* (the full moon). We agree that each step of our journey not only extends into the world around us, but also into the world within each of us. Traveling gives you the time needed to reflect before planning for future endeavors.

We enjoy the lights of the city, followed by dinner and music at an Irish pub before settling in at our hotel. While enjoying that English cup of tea, we review our day. Lou recalls that we never saw Craigdarroc Castle in the center of Victoria. We wish we had at least one more day to explore by bike, but we have made reservations for the next night in the city across the water, Vancouver.

The next morning we hustle to the bus station where we purchase two tickets to Vancouver. The bus actually drives onto the new ferry, Coastal Constellation, with its seven decks and many comfortable lounges surrounded by glass that never lets you forget that you are on a vessel, cruising through the San Juan Islands. Lou and I decide to treat ourselves to the first class buffet. We take a table by the window to enjoy the tasty food and spectacular views. As we approach the coast, we notice huge piles of yellow sulfur along the coastline and tankers galore. Yes, this does look like the largest Pacific port in the Americas.

We will soon depart the ferry on our coach and drive into Canada's third largest city with over two million inhabitants. This province is home to one–fourth of the ancient temperate rain forests left in the world, but they are far from the city we are visiting today. We are anxious to experience the natural beauty and mild climate Vancouver boasts year round. We depart the bus with plenty of energy and excitement. We are immediately enchanted as we roll our bags along the paths, bordering the waterfront, to our next hotel. The city has an assortment of massive modern skyscrapers and lots of green space surrounded by the gleaming waters of the Puget Sound.

Already we can tell the Vancouverites are active outdoor enthusiasts: bikers, runners, boaters and dog walkers. They clutter the paths and share their warmth and zest for life. Our hotel is miles from the bus station, but we find ourselves enjoying every step on this mild fall afternoon. We finally find our home-away-from-home in a residential area, a few blocks from the water. At first glance, we look at the each other and Lou says, "You are bound to get one dud when you make hotel reservations on-line."

We go inside to check in and see that our little neighborhood hotel is comfortable and conveniently located close to restaurants, bike shops and trails. We decide it is not that bad a choice after all.

We always seem to go for ambiance when choosing a restaurant in a new location, and tonight is no exception. We walk into a classy, two-story seafood restaurant and know this is not where we want to dine this late in the day, but we decide to stay and enjoy a few appetizers and glass of wine. Later, while strolling along the public beach, we notice several interesting things: first of all, the beach is lined with tree trunks, placed end to end so people can sit and enjoy the view, listen to the strolling musicians or even make a fire to take the chill off. Secondly, we spot a skunk on the pedestrian path. He dashes in and out among the people without any movement or comment from anyone. We even point out the little black and white animal to one couple sitting on a bench. They seem to be unaffected.

The evening is young, but we are ready to walk back to our room. We see just how quiet this little corner of the world really is. It meets all expectations and we wake, rested and ready, to tackle a new day in the city of Vancouver, British Columbia.

At breakfast the next morning, we meet Fridge, a retired teacher, who now makes a living as one of the strolling minstrels we saw last night at the beach. He is treating himself to a grand breakfast, thanks to a generous tip he received from a fan. We share travel stories while waiting for our meals. He shows us a photo of the antique car he uses to take people on sightseeing trips around the city. He tells us about some famous people who have been his clients. We decline as we have our hearts set on seeing Stanley Park by bicycle. We walk about six blocks where we find many shops from which to choose our rental bikes. As usual, the shop owners insist that we take the bike helmets and say, "It's the law!"

The park trail is only a few blocks away. I love it immediately. This is my idea of a perfect spot to ride bikes - paved path, away from highway traffic and noise and a photo-op around every bend. Our first stop, about two blocks into the ride, is Lost Lagoon. I keep in mind that Lou never wanted to miss an attraction along the way on his first journey just because he was on the bike. By the end of the day, I have a feeling he will let me know that his pace then was a bit more upbeat than it was today with me in tow. Not once, however, do I get the feeling that Lou would prefer to be traveling solo on his bike as he did thirteen years ago. I am relieved.

We follow the sea wall, past the old rowing club building and lighthouse. I imagine that a bit of boasting takes place among the chaps who spend their time crewing and drinking gin together behind those walls.

Totem Park is our next stop. We lock up our bikes and stroll around the circle with the other tourists, admiring the carvings and the legends depicted in each Totem carved by one of the tribe members of the Coastal First Nation. Originally, the First Nation people lived in villages along the coast. They built their homes using large cedar planks. The interior of the houses had beams and posts which were often carved and painted to tell the family story. In some coastal areas, the posts were placed outside their houses. One Totem, in which I am particularly interested, is carved by Ellen Neel, who became the first Northwest Coastal woman carver. This sculpture had a thunderbird at the top and a raven carved at the bottom, with other figures including a man, frog and killer whale in the middle area of the pole. It was on loan by the University of British Colombia; it was carved in 1955. While reading the information posted in the park, we discover that because of unfavorable West Coast weather conditions, all the Stanley Park's original totem poles now sit safely preserved in museums.

I am surprised that my bottom is not tired after riding a few hours, but guess the off-and-on stops make a trip like this more doable. I never do figure out how Lou never seems to complain or tire when he is on a bike. He is truly in his element.

The tide goes out; The Girl in the Wet Suit sculpture in the bay almost appears to be on shore as we approach and stop to take a few photos. The statue was erected about 200 meters off-shore in 1972. It was a gift to the Vancouver Park Department from the sculptor, Elek Imredy, from Budapest, Hungry. The statue represents Vancouver's dependence on the sea.

Each of the principal points of interest along the trail is well marked. We are getting a historical tour each time we stop to read and, of course, to take more photos. I am intrigued at the dozens of piles of stacked rocks or cairns out on the beach at English Bay at low tide. I park my bike and climb over the sea wall, eager to make one of my own and wish I could fill my back pack with these smooth stones.

Note to Self: "Let's make a reflecting stream from our spa area to the Chichen Itza fountain and add some extra special rocks gathered on future trips."

Wouldn't these stones be perfect for a warm stone massage? I had the pleasure of a gift of one of these massages performed by our next-door neighbor in Vail. I remember how she said when she was in massage school, she purchased an expensive collection of smooth stones to perform the procedure on her clients. When the stones arrived by mail, they were exactly like the ones she could have collected from the beach beside her back yard on the Massachusetts coast. It is way out of the question to collect these to add to our carry-on luggage so a photo will have to suffice. I know that we will not be able to find smooth stones in our back yard in Mexico where the stones are jagged limestone.

Around the bend, our eyes are drawn to something pink on the rocks at the edge of the water. We are delighted to see giant starfish, an octopus and miles of mussels. The strangest sight makes us stop, ponder, then giggle as we watch the sea gulls munching on three-inch wide starfish which protrude from both sides of their mouths.

The Lionsgate Bridge is often in view. We marvel at this suspension bridge, built in 1938 by the Guinness family (of Irish beer fame). They, and other British investors, had a need to reach the large tracts of land which they were anxious to develop on the north shore of Vancouver. One of the workers, on the bridge project in the early 1900's, described the structure as light and graceful, resembling a spider's web on a sunny morning. This is a sight we know well as our B & B, *La Selva Mariposa*, is located in a tropical jungle. With each morning stroll, we take time to admire the work of the spiders which have built their webs during the night.

The foot and bike traffic picks up as we get closer to the urban area. We realize it is lunch hour. We pass an interesting children's water park which is closed for the season. It surprises us that we see so many seniors on bikes. We talk about this as being one of those special cities we think we could actually live in. There are bike lanes over major bridges, even in the busiest parts of the city. We pedal towards Burrard Bridge, admiring all the cool sport cars and classic autos parked on every corner. We cross the bridge and know we have made a good choice when we see all the colorful market stalls on Granville Island. We are enchanted with the landscaping of apartment buildings and houses along the way. Lou and I are aware that we have been gifted with clear days for our trip to the Pacific Northwest. We know that the green trees and brilliantly colored flowers and plants could only grow in an area where rain is plentiful.

The public Farmers Market, under the bridge, is open from 9 a.m. until 7 p.m. seven days a week as are the over one hundred stores and restaurants which flourish in this popular tourist destination. While sampling a homemade potpie from one of the market booths on the waterfront, we enjoy watching the mini-tug boats shuffling people on and off Granville Island and the neighboring ports of call. We purchase some colorful berries for an afternoon snack and snap many photos of the plump, brightly colored vegetables that line the market stalls. You are fully aware that this is harvest season. The Pacific Northwest has been blessed by Mother Nature with rich soil and plenty of rainfall.

Note to Self: "We have to plant a garden rich with herbs, plump tomatoes, colorful peppers, tangy arugula and crunchy lettuce when we return to Tulum."

We have tried to grow these things in our kitchen garden, but each year, the heat has quickened the growing process and we never seem prepared for this. We planted our garden in raised beds built from concrete blocks on top of Lou's woodworking shop and the adjoining car port in hopes of keeping out nocturnal animals and discouraging our own dogs, who love to dig. This year we will let our Mayan gardener help with the planting. Perhaps we will learn a thing or two. We will also try to plant an herb garden in a partially shaded area, hoping to keep it growing into the late spring and on into summer.

We head toward the science center and lose the bike path in a warehouse district. Before long, we are back at the bridge where there are very well-marked bike entrances and exits. At the summit, I discover that I am a bit out of breadth; we stop for a magnificent panoramic view of the city of Vancouver below. "Look," Lou says, "There is the bike path we lost track of in the warehouse district. It would have been a great ride along the water, but I don't imagine you want to backtrack?" All I could do was shake my head.

We return the bikes and find a chic restaurant with a sea view for our afternoon cocktail and chat with two ladies and their tiny dog in a purse. They are going to visit friends, taking a small seaplane to a little Island in the bay. Now that sounds like a fun weekend get-away!

Later that night, while dining at a neighborhood Italian restaurant, we talk about this phase of our life as a time to seize the opportunity if it is in reach. We tell each other not to have second thoughts about how tomorrow's Sea to Sky train trip, aboard the golden dome car, is going to put a dent in our travel budget, but we both know it is something Lou has long dreamed of doing and we cannot let this moment slip by. We have made a reservation at the posh Fairmont Hotel in Whistler. We are already dreaming about being in the midst of a ski area once again. We know the town will be in tip-top condition, as the area readies for the 2010 Winter Olympics in February.

In the morning, a bus takes us from the Fairmont Hotel near #1 Canada Place to the depot. We board our luxurious train. The literature, on the Vancouver to Whistler rail passage, highlights the fact that it is a green operation. They recycle materials left in the cars, have retention tanks to handle waste on board and even donate excess food to the poor. Yes, another reason why this adventure is a good choice!

We are presented with a great view of the Lionsgate Bridge as we travel through the forests of North Vancouver and pass the area where the Guinness Estate is located. Many homes are precariously built, along the rocky cliffs, with the river rushing below. I follow the train map as the announcer fills us in on historical and geological information of interest, while the friendly wait-staff begin serving our breakfast on fine china. After breakfast, it doesn't surprise me that between Howe Sound, a glacially carved inlet or fjord, and Porteau Cove, my eyelids get heavy and I stare at the glass dome. It reminds me of the halocline effect of fresh and salt seawater mixing that you observe when swimming in the magical *cenotes* near our home in the Yucatan Peninsula of Mexico. Lou soon nudges me and lets me know this is no time for a nap as more peek-a-boo views are around every curve.

I perk up when I hear the conductor mention that, during a huge restoration of the old copper mine at Britannia Beach, the 18,000 panes of glass in the mine had been installed individually. That would keep our little crew in Macario Gomez working for an entire year. During the 1930s, this copper mine was the largest in the British Empire.

As we pass Brackendale, which is the largest bald eagle sanctuary in Canada, we spot one of these gorgeous creatures soaring over the treetops and then darting down toward the Cheakamus River, where the glacial water flows clear and green. The steep rocky slopes are contained by using gunnite, a spray, and a web of wires to keep the rocks from tumbling down.

Before long, we are able to see a hint of the Coast Mountain Range, which forms part of the larger Pacific coast ranges stretching down the western coast of North America from Alaska to Mexico.

When the train announcer tells the story of the Salish First Nation about the famous monolithic Black Tusk Peak looming in the distance, I think of Ellen Neel's Totem Pole, with the Thunderbird at the top which we had recently seen in Stanley Park. I realize I did not know what this winged creature signifies to Salish people. The Thunderbird was believed to be the creator and controller of the elements and spirits. When he flew, the flapping of his wings caused the thunder and the flashing of his eyes caused the lightening. He lived in the highest of mountains and was both feared and revered by the people of the region. Now, as I glance at this distant peak, I am able to envision the mythical Thunderbird in its place.

We are awestruck as the train climbs higher and higher toward our destination, the Whistler ski area. We find that the Cheakamus Canyon, Brandywine Falls and Alpha Lake can be easily photographed from our golden dome car. This is a three-hour tour which could have turned into a full-day trip, if we had been driving and stopping to snap each photo. I do recall that Lou said it was difficult to pull over to take a photo safely on the Sea to Sky Highway, when he made this drive with a friend thirteen years ago. I also remember wondering why he did not ride his bike up to this ski area, as he had done from Vail to Steamboat Springs, at the beginning of his original bike adventure. Now, I can truly understand.

We are always intrigued by the experiences of other innkeepers. When Lou and I moved to Mexico in 2003, we felt like pioneers who had many obstacles to overcome and hurdles to jump through before we opened our bed and breakfast. But, Myrtle and Alex Phillips' adventure, traveling by ferry, stagecoach and finally on foot to Alta Lake to open the Rainbow Lodge in 1914, made our journey along the *Mariposa Trail* pulling our 4,000-pound trailer with a GMC Suburban sound like a picnic. Even in its rustic innocence, the Rainbow Lodge became the most popular summer destination west of the Rocky Mountains fifty years before Whistler became a ski resort. Hopefully, in fifty years, when Tulum is the heart of the tourist industry on the Riviera Maya, *La Selva Mariposa* will still be the top B & B to stay at while touring the nearby Mayan ruins.

Lou looks over at me and tells me that four businessmen had the foresight to develop Whistler as a potential site for the 1966 Winter Olympics. Whistler did not get chosen as the site that year, but the mountain did open and since, it has been in constant competition with Vail, Aspen and Sun Valley for the rating as #1 Ski Resort in North America. I was shocked to hear that the town site was built on a former garbage dump, proving anything is possible. The sister ski area right next door, Blackcomb, opened soon after as North America's only mile-high mountain Today, both ski areas work together co-operatively, even though they are two separate business entities. The 2010 Winter Olympics are scheduled to take place at Whistler and neighboring ski mountains, so the original investors and their families must be elated that their dream is finally coming true.

When Lou visited the Whistler/Blackcomb ski areas thirteen years ago, he was guided by his friend, Michelle, who was familiar with the area. I am thrilled in turn to be in the company of someone who knows his way around. The villages are easy to maneuver. A free bus circles the area regularly, stopping at the many covered bus shelters along the way, even in the off-season. There are well- marked paths, offering another way to get around on foot. We mix it up; take a bus to start, then find a trail and leisurely walk from one section of the village to the other, enjoying the views of the snow-capped mountains in the distance with no shortage of greenery and flowers in every direction. A milky-jade-colored stream slices its way through the countryside, carrying icy water from the glaciers above us. A mountain-bike race is in progress. We pass many young competitors, coated in a layer of mud caused by the off-and-on rain, which is typical in this part of the country. The streets feel lively with this mix of tourists and locals, enjoying both the mountains and the village.

The morning seems to melt seamlessly into the afternoon and we realize we are starving. It is easy to find a spot to have lunch at one of the restaurants with an outside deck for some tasty food and people-watching. The street life in Whistler reminds us of Beaver Creek, Colorado. After lunch, the now-sunny skies and balmy fall temperatures keep us moving along. We dip in and out of shops along the mall. I am drawn to the fleece clothing that I was accustomed to wearing when living in Vail. I purchase a vest, even though I expect it will not get much wear in the tropics, but for now, I will need another layer to take the chill off tonight.

We end our tour of both villages back at our hotel hot tub, sipping my new favorite drink, Bloody Caesar, the specialty of the house. The sun setting early in the mountains, followed by decreasing temperatures, seems to empty the pools and decks of the sun worshipers. We find ourselves in our own private Jacuzzi. As we talk about our day, I say to Lou, "I loved walking all over the ski villages. It seemed to give me a sense of intimacy with these two soon-to-be-famous towns which will swarm with thousands of people from all over the world at the upcoming Winter Olympics (February, 2010). I am happy we got to see it before the World did. Now we can relive our memories in a few months when the surrounding scenery will be splashed all over the Internet and television."

I have a feeling his thoughts are elsewhere when I get no response.

Back in our room at the luxurious Fairmont Hotel overlooking the mountains, we have a hard time convincing each other we should go out to eat, but we are hungry and the price of room service is, not surprisingly, over-the-top. We actually never leave the hotel, and spend the next few hours in the hotel's popular lobby lounge. We find a table in front of the talented singer, order drinks and follow a few other guests over to the free-appetizer station. We copy-cat them, filling our plates with tasty snacks and, before we arrive back at our table, frosty mugs of beer are awaiting us. The lounge fills up. It seems like this is the in-spot in town. From the looks of the plates, piled high with appetizers, locals and tourists are here for the free food and entertainment as the slowly sip the over-priced cocktails.

Later that night, we fall into the big luxurious bed without a thought of when we will wake.

In the morning, we cannot resist returning to the spa's hot tubs. Because the skies have opened up and drenched the mountain landscape, and yesterday's sun is tucked behind the clouds, the spa in its indoor pool and Jacuzzis are packed to the brim. The steam room has yet to be discovered by the crowd so we slip in there before going back to our room. We have arranged a late checkout. The hotel keeps our bags a little longer while we go out for breakfast and a walk in the chilly drizzling rain - a far cry from the warm *chippi-chippi* rain we have in Mexico.

We are scheduled to take a bus back to Vancouver at 3 p.m. and are pleased that this choice will give us a completely different view of the countryside from the train ride up the slope. We feel we are much closer to the water by bus and, after the first half hour on this twisting road, we wonder about the bus driver's comment about being able to spot gray whales and orcas everyday from his perch at the front of the coach. How could he take his eyes off the road for even a second? Well, to our disappointment, no whales today.

We take a bus from downtown Vancouver to West Vancouver, where the bus drops us off a block away from our next hotel, in an area shaded with large pine trees. We are a bit isolated from most everything, but have specifically chosen this location because of its proximity to Grouse Mt. Ski Area which Lou visited on his premier journey. We inquire about a good restaurant in the neighborhood. The manager points in the direction of the suspension bridge, shadowing the water in the distance. We are within walking distance of a spectacular restaurant, with a huge wait staff of young, beautiful people. The clients keep pouring into the restaurant, which has a patio and a dozen televisions tuned into different sporting events. It feels like local happy hour. The mood is contagious.

After dinner, we decide to take a walk in the chilly evening air. We find ourselves walking across the tall Lionsgate Bridge towards downtown Vancouver until the height makes the butterflies in my stomach do flip-flops. We turn around and take in the lights of the city across the bridge and the woodland community we are sleeping in tonight.

By morning, the weather has turned cold for our thin blood and we bundle up. I am grateful to have a soft fleece vest to zip on over my layers. Lou asks at the desk about taxis and buses, but the clerk is new to the area and has no idea if Grouse is open or what transportation is available. We decide to just walk on the road toward Grouse Mt. Ski Area in hopes of finding some sort of transportation going our way. We are in a very residential area; there are no bus stops or taxis and it is cold and damp.

We were told by several travelers we met during our vacation, to stay away from the high priced tourist trap of Capilano Suspension Bridge, a few miles from where we are staying. We find out later, to our disappointment, that it is one of the must-see spots in the world.

"Lou, how come you did not see the suspension bridge when you were traveling solo on your Jamison Coda?"

"I suspect it was too expensive. Since my budget was dwindling at this stage of my trip, I had to pick and choose what to spend my money on. Places with a hefty entrance fee were the first to be eliminated. "

We did find out later that Vancouver's North Shore Mountains, with breathtaking old-growth forests, consist of three different mountain peaks: Mt. Seymour, Mt. Cyprus and Grouse Mt. Today, the latter two areas are busy preparing for the Olympics, only a few months away and mountain operations are pretty well closed down after Labor Day. During the summer, there are sky rides, zip lines and chairlift rides. These ski areas have a total of only six chair lifts and fifty-three downhill ski runs, but often have decent ski conditions, even though very little snow ever falls in the city of Vancouver which is at sea level. The closures make us realize that there are some advantages to traveling during the high season when everything is functioning.

In spite of a few glitches in getting around in Northwest Vancouver, we have become very comfortable with the public transportation in Canada as well as Washington State. We are pleased that we did not rent a car.

twenty-one

The bus takes us to Seattle. We arrive rested and ready to explore the city before boarding a ferry to Bainbridge Island. Lou points out the monorail, Space Needle and the new architecturally whimsical Music Project building, in the shadows. Lou remembers that this area once appeared to be farther away and much more isolated from the downtown area. It is Saturday and the city seems a bit deserted as we roll our bags up and down the hills until we reach the waterfront. My husband, and tour guide, has an amazing sense of direction so I never hesitate to follow his lead. I feel a sense of excitement because I am in a new city, one I have always dreamed of exploring. We have made plans to have Jackie and Rich, who hosted Lou on his earlier expedition, meet us at the ferry across the Puget Sound in Bainbridge, so we don't dawdle. We plan to spend a day later this week exploring the city so the impulse to explore the Pike Street Market will have to wait.

The street life, near the waterfront, is lively and jammed with tourists and locals alike. There are people signing up for harbor tours; others waiting in line at the aquarium or buying flowers from venders, as they nibble on snacks, sold at small storefronts.

As we board the ferry, a young girl with a bicycle gives us some background information on riding in Seattle. She lives on Bainbridge Island and travels back and forth by ferry, then uses her bike to get to work and run errands in the city. We find out later that Rich, who works in the fishing industry, also uses this back and forth technique to get to work in Seattle during the summer. He parks his car in a leased spot, near the ferry on Bainbridge and, on most days, takes the bike, rather than the car, across the Sound.

This charming young lady politely listens to Lou's passionate stories from his pedaling journey thirteen years ago when he was turning fifty. She manages to squeeze in some information about our next destination, across the water. She tells us that this island city is known for its arts community and even has its own performing arts center and arts and crafts gallery, featuring local artists. I perk up when I hear the island is home to many well known authors like David Guterson and Rebecca Wells.

I am enchanted to see that Bainbridge Island is just as Lou described it and Jackie and Rich are just as welcoming as ever. Lou is relieved that these two old friends remember the guy he has become, rather than the one they knew more than twenty years ago when alcohol and drugs spoke for him. I also knew our hosts during this period in Vail, but seem to have forgotten a few things about our friendship; like my being a guest at their wedding. I insist on seeing their wedding album and, sure enough, there I was in the photos, smiling and enjoying being a part of their special day. Jackie said she did not recall any other guests ever asking to see their wedding album from the late 1980s.

The deck of the house looks like a sports shop with drying scuba gear, racquets and athletic shoes of every variety. Right away we ask about the farmhouse they once offered to Lou to live in when he passed by over a decade ago. They have torn it down and a large green-space with towering trees now makes up the landscape in front. I still remember Jackie's passion for horses and see the barn and tack room next to the house. She has sold the horses and bought two goats to keep the back-forty trimmed. A bocce ball court has taken over the area that once was the riding arena. I even get a glimpse of the prospering garden behind the barn. Tomorrow we are promised a complete tour, but now it is time to get settled and have dinner. Guess what is on the menu? Salmon, of course!

We know just how many years have passed since Lou's first visit when she tells us that their son, Austin, is an engineering student at the state university and their daughter, Ana, is heading off in a few weeks to begin her university career. Jackie and Rich are taking a scuba diving class as they will soon be traveling to Bali. We swap stories from Lou's earlier trip to this magnificent country. I have a feeling that they will come visit us one day in Mexico to get more diving experience under their belts. It is easy to see that Jackie is still a sports enthusiast; she has swapped skiing for scuba and horseback riding for cycling.

Their hospitality is over-whelming and we find so much to talk about. Jackie no longer works in Seattle; she has moved her law office to Bainbridge Island. She is taking tomorrow off to show us around.

Rich has chores to catch up on at home. We agree to meet later for a tour of the Kitsap Peninsula. Today the weather is threatening, yet no noticeable rain ever falls. Jackie, Lou and I take off to see the Island and the coastal beaches; the World War II bunkers, one of the Island's most beautiful gardens; the local golf course; and, finally, Restoration Point. The latter is the site where Captain George Vancouver sailed his ship, HMS Discovery, into Puget Sound in 1792 and, in 1841, it was here that the Squamish First Nation ceded Bainbridge Island and other lands to the United States government. Surprisingly, it wasn't until the 1900s that the Island land was cleared and farms began to pop up throughout Bainbridge. Because of the mild temperatures and abundance of rainfall, Bainbridge Island was ideal for growing small fruit trees, hops and strawberries. Jackie continues to share fascinating bits of local history, including the great influence the Japanese and Filipinos had on the development of Bainbridge Island. Their strawberry farms were the benchmark of the industry in their day. Jackie and Rich's home was once a strawberry farm; in fact, the area where they live is known as Strawberry Hill.

During World War II, the Japanese-American residents of Bainbridge Island were the first to be sent to internment camps. They were held by the United States government through the duration of the war for fear of espionage. After World War II, as their farms had been confiscated, much of the farming was discontinued. During this time the lumber industry grew; by late 1800s, Port Blakely housed the world's largest lumber mill. The shipbuilding industry also prospered after the war. We stop to browse in the shopping areas of Port Madison in the northern part of the Island which were once a popular commercial area in the late 1800s for smart Seattle connoisseurs.

We notice that historic places are well-marked on the Island. There are many fascinating stops along our tour. Jackie had obviously given this tour many times to visitors and was proud to show off her little

Island. We talk about using their bikes to go for a ride the next day, but she reminds us of the steep Island terrain. I know this is more of a ride than I am prepared to tackle, so we make plans to take a hike through the near-by Grand Forest. Jackie says that we can go on-line to the Island's web site and find the latest maps for hiking trails. It also gives the best bike routes and kayak launches. It is easy to see that this community supports active transportation.

Before we leave for our afternoon tour, Jackie makes a call and gets a personal tour for Lou and me to Islandwood on Monday. She can tell that we are enchanted with natural environments, gardening and sustainable building materials; and she knows schools are still a passion of mine.

Later that afternoon we pick up Rich and leave Bainbridge by way of the Agate Pass Bridge to the Kitsap Peninsula. We proceed over the Hood Canal Bridge to the Olympic Peninsula to visit the little town of Port Townsend. Our first stop is an old military base, Ft. Worden, where the movie *An Officer and a Gentleman* was filmed. This site is now managed by the State Park System and the officer's homes and barracks are rented to the public. It is popular for family reunions and large gatherings. While sitting in the car, looking at the water, Lou spots a whale at three o'clock in the Puget Sound.

We drive around the waterfront before heading into town and walk around admiring the Victorian architecture and interesting shops. We have a hard time deciding where to have a meal, but finally settle on an old English teahouse whose ambiance turns out to be a perfect ending for our day with friends.

The next morning, we walk to a trail in the Grand Forest near their home and enjoy a quiet hike among the vast hypnotic, towering trees in a cool forest which couldn't be more different from the environment we call home in the Yucatan Peninsula. Yes, we still have tall trees left in Mexico's Mayan jungles, but because they are continually being cut without replanting them, the jungle canopy is getting sparser and sparser. A walk in a tropical jungle, on most days, will leave you wiping the perspiration from your brow rather than leaving you feeling refreshed.

After our hike, we hustle to keep our appointment for the tour at Islandwood. This is a non-profit, outdoor learning center on two hundred and fifty-five acres, founded in 2001, to provide environmental education to fourth, fifth and sixth graders from Seattle and neighboring towns. We are anxious to see the facility attended by 4,000 children each year. Children stay, up to four days at a time, engaging in hands-on, integrated learning experiences in science, technology and the arts. We find out on our tour that the facility, with space for 175 guests, is also used for corporate meetings, conferences, family reunions and weddings. These are used to raise funds to support scholarships for low-income children attending the overnight programs.

Shannon, our guide, greets us at the entrance to the Great Room. Upon entering, we are astounded to see the hugest wooden beam incorporated into the truss system that either of us has ever seen. Shannon tells us that the ninety-two-foot Douglas fir beam was originally milled at Port Blakely's lumber mill 120 years ago. The beam was found in a mine in Montana. It was donated to Islandwood, if they could move it. It took two flatbed trucks to get it to Seattle. The Columbia Helicopter Service offered to donate their time, if the beam weighed less than 9,000 pounds. As luck would have it, the mammoth hunk of wood weighed in at 8,864 pounds. It has become the showpiece of the center. A children's book, *The Tree That Came Home,* tells the story of this tree's journey. When I heard the story, I knew I could not resist purchasing a copy for my library.

We spend over two hours touring the grounds and buildings. We catch glimpses of children engaged in the outdoor classrooms, learning the difference between marshes and bogs from atop a tree house or on a manually powered child-size raft. We can imagine them walking in the early morning mist observing a family of deer nibbling under the tall pine trees. We are lucky enough to see an owl flying through the forest as we cross the suspension bridge. We know that there are other animals scattered about the landscape, each with its own perfect camouflage. Lou is fascinated at the sustainable materials, such as bamboo flooring, used in the construction of the buildings. I am busy snapping photos of interesting ways they are experimenting with growing vegetables in their garden. We know we will add a few more items on our to-do list for *La Selva Mariposa*, once we leave today.

Note to Self: "Mix flowers with vegetables in your garden."

We walk out of the greeting center towards the car, with Islandwood's vision statement ringing in our ears: "We envision a future in which all people view themselves as lifelong learners and share a bond of stewardship for the environment, for their community and for each other." We know that this little backdoor tour was not on Lou's list of places to return to, but we are both inspired by what we have seen and hope that we will use some of the ideas to make our little piece of the earth more beautiful while respecting Mother Nature as our mentor.

The next day we depart on an early morning ferry to explore the city of Seattle. We find that you do not have to purchase a ticket from Bainbridge to Seattle, only the other way around. As the ship slips out of the harbor, I contemplate this world of water that surrounds us; I soak up this image in my mind. Since Lou toured the city on foot the first time, he has a strong sense of the highlights he wants to share with me. Again, I am feeling like a traveler devouring a new place for only a short time.

The sights, sounds and smells of the vast Pike Place Market are all that I had imagined. The bins are heaped with tomatoes and multi-colored peppers. The dahlias are the largest I have ever seen. I won't soon forget the bouquets with primary red, hot pink, brilliant yellow and dashes of purple flowers - all tied together and perched in a bin of water for less than $10. A crowd gathers around a fishmonger's stand as the actors/clerks toss the fish to one another, shouting a chant as they have done for over fifty years. The people in the market are warm, have big smiles and are eager to greet you. We find a cheese stall selling home-made, artisan cheese and order a three-cheese *panini* which we eat standing up at a counter.

We leave the bustling waterfront behind and head uphill. Lou points out the Seattle Museum of Art and the skyscraper where Jackie worked when he first visited Seattle. We take one of the free downtown buses and proceed to Pioneer Square where he and Jackie visited together. The energy here is contagious. I am intrigued by the underground tours into the catacombs of the city, but we decide there is more to see topside. Besides, the tour is full and we would have to wait another hour for the next one to begin. We discover tiny ethnic shops which speak of the diverse communities living in and around Seattle. We find a store with beautiful Asian clothing and accessories. Lou finds an elegant black shirt which will be perfect for our last night's dinner with Jackie and Rich.

We breeze in and out of children's stores on the main street, looking for a polka-dot shirt for our grandson. My daughter is expecting her second baby in a few months and Kaidan says he will be a big brother when he has a polka-dot shirt. We find one in an exclusive children's store for $45, but decide we will buy a white tee-shirt and fabric markers. Together, we will make the special shirt to signal this life-changing event in our grandson's life.

This, like most days on our vacation, has fallen into a rhythm which keeps us moving at a smooth and steady pace until we decide to stop at a quaint tea shop to rest and sample tea served in beautiful china cups. We decide we have seen all the points of interest Lou has intended to share with me, along with a few new sights. We agree it is time to return to our home-away-from-home. We linger at the waterfront before heading into the ferry terminal to purchase our ticket back to Bainbridge Island to spend our last evening with a quiet dinner at home with Jackie and Rich.

The day arrives when we are to leave. We take the ferry, one last time, from Bainbridge Island back to Seattle, a city perched on the edge of a country. We wheel our bags first uphill, then walk below street level to the metro station. We purchase our tickets, study our route and discover we will have to make only one transfer. We board a bus to the airport. We are told that by February 2010, when the Winter Olympics comes to near-by Canada, the last leg of the rail system will be complete all the way to the airport. Bravo to the developers and engineers behind the fantastic public transportation system operating in Seattle and the neighboring communities!

While waiting for our plane to Denver for the next part of our trip, to visit friends and family, we are both feeling satisfied to have made this journey to the Pacific Northwest. This trip has given us the drive to continue to break new ground and seek new adventures as we tread on this fragile earth. In a few more weeks, we will be returning to *La Selva Mariposa* in the Mayan jungle of Mexico, where we have created an oasis for people from all over the world to rest, rejuvenate and share their stories. We know we have some great new stories and images to add to the travel journals in our minds.

SOUTH OF THE BORDER

twenty-two

True to character, when we return home, we take out our *To-Do* list and start to make plans.

> *Note to Self*: "Let's make a reflecting stream from our spa area to the Chichen Itza fountain and fill the stream with smooth stones and some extra special rocks found on our journeys to come."

Lou returns to Mexico a couple of weeks before me to get started on this project so that it will be finished by the time my family visits in early November. When I arrive home, I ask him to tell me how he created this new addition to our little oasis.

"I pulled out my surveyor's eye level and checked the altitude drop between the spa and the Chichen Itza fountain, which turned out to be about twelve inches. This did not leave much room to make a babbling brook, hence the reflecting stream. It was a tedious task to keep the elevations correct, as the raised bed is about ninety feet long, but through trial and error, the stream, lined with smooth river stones, finally flowed. To get the additional sound I desired, I had to put a by-pass pipe in from the spa and build another waterfall outside the bedroom window."

I predict there will be many nights at *La Selva Mariposa* where guests will be happily lulled to sleep by the sound of these flowing waters.

Note to Self: "Make a greenhouse at *La Selva Mariposa* for growing flowers." Within minutes we scratch this one off the list and add, "Buy as many flowers of one color as we can to fill our new flower beds, being constructed while we are on vacation."

One rainy day in November, Lou hooks up the trailer that we had originally towed from Colorado to Mexico and drives toward Valladolid in search of flowers. He returns with as many as he could find. These, alone, will not fill one of the beds at Butchart Gardens. We are delighted to at least have made a start. We cross this item off our list, all the while being optimistic that the flowers will propagate and bring joy to those who pass by.

Note to Self: "We have to plant a garden rich with herbs, plump tomatoes, colorful peppers, tangy arugula and crunchy lettuce when we return to Tulum."

When we were in Colorado, we visited many different plant nurseries and purchased packets of seeds to grow dill, basil, cilantro, parsley, sweet corn, bell and peppers. We found many different varieties of tomatoes and lettuce mixtures to bring back with us. While we were gone, Jose, our gardener, prepared the gardens by tilling them and adding a fill of the mixture from our compost pit. We were aware that, along with the compost, we were getting seeds of papaya and tomatoes which may take root as well. We already had a fourteen-foot papaya tree growing in the rooftop gardens. It was started from a seed buried in the compost. We had previously put in a watering system. From what we could see, there has been little rain since we left six weeks ago. So we were good to go.

Note to Self: "Mix flowers with vegetables in your garden."

This is a natural process for the Mayan farmers. Jose adds marigolds, baby mums, sunflowers and some wild flowers to the vegetable gardens along the drive. He also plants some alongside the vegetables in our rooftop garden. The baby plants are slow to germinate because of the intense heat, but by early November, the long awaited rains start and there are many downpours which flood our baby sprouts and make it difficult for them to take hold. The strong ones survive; some even love the abundance of water.

I am thrilled to have a rich kitchen garden all winter. I am very proud to announce, with each dish we serve our guests, that it includes home grown tomatoes, herbs etc. Lou's famous tours of the property, a highlight for our visitors to *La Selva Mariposa*, always end with a visit to the rooftop gardens. We often get tips from guests who are seasoned gardeners such as: don't get discouraged if something does not grow well; try again next year. Advice taken! This is just what we plan to do.

twenty-three

When the excitement of returning home settles and we are back into a groove which allows some time to ourselves, I begin to reflect on the trip we have just taken and how our recent travels are related to the first half of this book, *Shifting Gears: A Journey of Reinvention*.

Lou walks past the patio where I am sitting with Jose and Julio, our key workers, while describing some needed changes in the gardens. I realize how confident he has grown since his youth, since the bike trip through the west and even since we completed building *La Selva Mariposa*. He can speak to these two young men and his crews, which have totaled as many as sixty Mayans at a time, in a combination of Spanglish, hand signals and a sense of trust he has built up with them over time.

I begin to think about my Polish-American husband and what I have learned about him from his life stories which unfolded as he pedaled from Steamboat Springs, Colorado to the Pacific Northwest and down the California coast, before returning to Colorado in 1995.

He found adventure each day even though it was not the principle objective of the trip. Being with Lou means life will be one adventure after another. I am beginning to see adventure as a spirit which can be present anywhere as long as you open your heart to these new experiences and keep fear at bay. Our move from Colorado to Mexico many years later was the adventure of a lifetime!

On the 1995 bicycle journey to the Pacific Northwest, Lou was looking for a new place to put down roots, sometimes, with me in mind and sometimes, alone in the event that things did not work out with us. He used his creative genius to evaluate each possibility and, in the end, he returned to Colorado to make a life with Ailish and me. At the time, neither of us realized that we both had the same dream - to build a little pre-retirement business in a warm location near a beautiful beach. Together, we explored the possibility until it became a reality.

Many people say Lou is a Renaissance man - a man with ideas before his time. Often, his visionary ideas did not pan out. Just finding a little piece of paradise to set down new roots was only part of his hopes and dreams for the future. This had to be a place where his creative skills would be useful. His efforts would finally result in a business venture which would bring both pride and stability to our lives. *La Selva Mariposa* has grown to be a unique and popular vacation destination in just five short years. The possibilities for expansion and creative projects are endless. Lou will never be at a loss for something to challenge his creative genius.

Lou had always been a loner, and was in his element when he was pedaling his Jamison Coda along the back roads of the west. Because he had just left our relationship that was teeter-tottering in mid-air, perhaps the option of living the next fifty years of his life alone or being settled in a warm, lasting partnership was more in the forefront of his mind than he realized at the time. But, he was surrounded by beautiful places to ride his bicycle and each day flowed evenly into the next. It was understandable to push the more serious thoughts about the future away, and focus on the moment. There would always be *mañana*. Little did he or anyone know that he would have a rich family life ten years later with a wife and grandchildren.

In past ventures, Lou's inability to reach the goals he set for himself lowered his self-confidence, but, as I recall from many of his early stories of days-gone-by in Vail and Aspen (racing down Vail Mountain to beat the gondola), he was perhaps aiming over-the-top. Setting unreachable expectations often result in loss of joy in your life from the stress you are carrying. I can see that he is now able to complete projects successfully; being aware of his limits. He now knows when to let others step in to help. The satisfaction he genders from this change brings a sense of peace to his life and mine.

Telling stories has always been a favorite pastime of my husband's, and as he traveled, he dazzled his hosts with stories from the road. At *La Selva Mariposa*, Lou has an outlet for his storytelling around the breakfast table. This brings out the gift-of-gab in many of our B & B guests.

The many hours Lou spends on his bicycle give him plenty of time to think. I wonder if he has finally re-configured his past or if there will always be some monsters lurking in the shadows. When I ask him what he thinks, he says, "I'm not sure I have the answer to that one, but I know I want my life to be my own, unencumbered by even my own shadow. I guess time will tell if any monsters reappear."

A few months later, while sitting beside one of the cascading waterfalls at *La Selva Mariposa* with my arm in a sling, I cannot help but laugh when I think about the fact that I broke my elbow in a cycling accident on the Coba' Road near our house. Here I am about to finish the last chapter of a book about a bicycle journey. How lucky Lou was not to have had a mishap like this when he was traveling so far from home.

As I begin to write in my notebook, Lou stops by on his afternoon rounds of the property. He sits down next to me. In the dim *siesta* light, he looks into my eyes and says, "Moe, I imagine you will soon be finished writing our story. I was hoping that I could include your hand-written manuscript, along with the original journals and photos from the bike trip in my white box. Since you will have some free time when the book is complete, would you mind making a CD of the photos we took on our Pacific Northwest trip? I want to save them also in my box of memories."

"I am touched, Lou, but recall once-upon-a-time when it was you at the computer making a music CD for our wedding. I wonder what happened to it."

"You are in luck, I saved a copy in the white box along with my favorite wedding picture of us, on the bridge leading from the house to the beach where all our guests were waiting until song #11, *All My Life*, by Linda Ronstadt and Aaron Neville began to play."

"My favorite song from the wedding CD was *Perhaps Love* by John Denver and Placido Domingo which was played when we released the live butterflies at the end of the ceremony. I know that, as the years pass, memory fades, but I can't imagine loosing any of the luster of that full-moon evening on Galveston Beach eight years ago."

The sheer beauty of our story gives me chills, and I know that, once again, I have created something which has allowed me to give back to someone I love; before letting it go and moving on to the next chapter of our life together.

"Lou, I am thrilled to once again have three things that will make me happy."

"I remember about the three things, Moe, but I am still trying to figure out what the third one is? Yes, you have someone to love and, thanks to my suggestion to make the CD, you have something to do, but what are you planning for the third thing; something to look forward to?"

"Well, I am thinking that we might have another cause for celebration when the book is published and in our hands. For sure we will need to take the white box out again and add the first copy to it."

"*Claro que si,*" responded my Polish-American-jack-of–all-trades husband.

APPENDIX

Lou Reflects

I want to include some important notations and figures so that I never forget just what I saw and accomplished on this eight-week solo bicycle journey in 1995, and what I want to remember for my next ride or return trip to the area.

What strikes me most when I review things in my mind is the fact that I upped my hourly speed from eight to twenty miles per hour the last day. Embarking on my solo bicycle journey at the beginning of fall was a little risky. I realize that I was amazingly lucky to have encountered mild temperatures overall, with a pleasant mix of clear blue and cloudy skies and only one day biking in the rain in a part of the country where moisture from above is a daily occurrence. I saw some of the most beautiful places in the north and western parts of our country and Canada, most of which I had not seen before. I made some new friends, renewed old friendships, and even found out that I had a couple less. I was relieved that I had no negative encounters with animals or people along the road; in fact, I was delighted that people of all ages seemed to open their hearts to this middle-age biker. I took about thirty rolls of film, and was able to keep friends and family abreast of my adventures through post cards. I found places worth seeing again: Glacier National Park; Whitefish, Montana; the California coast; Butchart Gardens; the city of Victoria, B.C., the San Juan Islands, including Roche Harbor, Doe Bay, Friday Harbor and

Vancouver Island. I would treasure revisiting all the wonderful friends who shared their homes and lives with me.

I wish that I had taken the time to travel up the western coast of Canada to the Pacific Rim National Park, and out to Tofino. I discovered that I had all the gear I needed for my first long journey, but will make changes for my next trip.

On the road while I was camping, protein bars worked well to keep hunger at bay until I got spoiled with all the good food at neighboring campground restaurants and dinners with my friends along the way. I managed to gain weight because of being fooled as to how many calories I was actually burning. I liked eating and camping at Lake Quinault, but that was because the Dasses brought everything you need to enjoy outdoor cooking over an open fire. Eating out is also part of meeting people, so I need to strike a balance.

I probably rode too many miles per day and should have stayed an extra day in places that were really beautiful and maybe a few less days at friend's houses, where I might have stayed too long.

I was also lucky to have vehicles to use in Montana at Ralph's, Jim's, Mark King's and Jackie's on Bainbridge and Dasse's in Oregon. It helped me see more of the areas painlessly.

I think the most unique experience I enjoyed was being a member of Ralph Ferraro's pit crew at the stock car races in Bozeman, Montana.

> *Note to Self:* When I do my next bicycle trip, I will need a lesson in bicycle repair and maintenance, a little cooking equipment, more money, or less restaurant food and, lastly, a companion.

I also was able to watch my stocks tumble, something I was hoping would pay for my trip but that didn't work out. I spent close to $3,000 in the eight weeks out, which works out to about $53 per day.

Expenses:
$200 train tickets
$150 bike repairs, etc.
$200 film, postcards etc.
$300 on campsites, motels
$ 80 ferries/ bus

$ 75 tourist related sightseeing
$ 2,000 food and entertainment

Total miles:
Bike 2,294
Car 350
Train 2,000
Bus 100

_____

Total: 4,744

Overnights:
Camping 24
Friend's homes 25
Hotels/hostels 5
Trains 2

_____

56 nights

Mileage milestones:
Most miles in a day 119
Least miles in a day 15

Bike breakdowns/problems:
Smith Bay, WA panniers rack
Bainbridge, WA 2 spokes
Daly City, CA 1 spoke
Big Sur, CA 1 spoke
Santa Barbara, CA 1 spoke
No flat tires!!!!

Most awesome sites:
Artist Point, Lower Falls, Yellowstone National Park
Glacier National Park
Butchart Gardens
Road to Whistler Ski area
Big Fork, Montana
Highway #1 California coast

Worst area for riding a bicycle:
Southern Wyoming
Between and around Lom Poc, CA to Santa Barbara

Favorite city I visited:
Victoria, B.C.

Cutest village I visited:
La Conner, WA.

Most scenic ride:
Monterey Peninsula